Discovering
PLACE-NAMES

John Field

Shire Publications Ltd

CONTENTS

ACKNOWLEDGEMENTS

Advice and information on particular names and problems have been given by the following, whose help is gratefully acknowledged: Mr John Dodgson (London), Mr Éamonn de hOir (Dublin), Professor Tomás Ó Maille (Galway) and the late Professor Melville Richards (Bangor).

Cover design by Ron Shaddock.

Printed in Great Britain by C. I. Thomas & Sons (Haverfordwest) Ltd, Press Buildings, Merlins Bridge, Haverfordwest, Dyfed.

1: NAMES AND MEANINGS

A natural curiosity about our environment includes, often enough, a desire to learn the meaning of names, whether of people or of places. Consulting an ordinary dictionary does not greatly help; the separate parts of **Bloomsbury** (Mx—now GL) or **Blindcrake** (Cu) seem to be words that the dictionary would include, but if we define them separately, we are no nearer the meaning of the place-name; and what could we do about a name like **Blencogo** (Cu)? An encyclopaedia sometimes obliges with the meaning of a name, but usually it confines what it says to geographical information about the place concerned. This book attempts to provide a brief explanation of a large number of place-names, but a further question may remain: how does anyone know?

If we were to try to solve the problem of **Blencogo,** we should probably argue something like this: the parts of this name represent no recognizable word, and so they have perhaps been altered, modified by the use of the name over a long period of time. Next, we might try to guess what the name had been altered from—and might indeed come up with some convincing suggestions—but would be left with the knowledge that anyone else's guess might be better than ours. A better idea would be to try to find evidence of what form or forms the name had taken in the past, and find where that information led us. This is what place-name investigators in fact try to do—trace the forms of the name back as far as possible and then inspect the early forms obtained. A knowledge of the early stages of the language or languages concerned will enable missing steps of the development to be traced, or suggest roots from which the name or its parts are ultimately derived. To the outsider, there is sometimes an incredible leap to what appears to be an unlikely conclusion, but the place-name scholar will always be prepared to explain the steps in his argument, the sound-changes that have occurred, the possible reasons for abrupt alterations, and so on. What must be lacking in a small book like the present one is the evidence of early forms by which the interpretations are arrived at. Occasionally one or two particularly interesting names can be singled out for a longer explanation, but for really full discussions of the names and their meanings recourse must be had to such works as the separate county surveys of the English Place-Name Society.

Blencogo appears to be one of a great number of composite names which contain elements from two languages. It is suggested that to an original Celtic name, *Blencog*, 'cuckoo hill', the Norse *haugr* 'mound' was added by a population who did not realise that the hill concerned already had that designation as part of its name. **Blindcrake** contains the same first element as **Blencogo**, *blaen*, 'top, summit', the second syllable being the British word *craig*, 'crag, rock', making the whole name 'craggy hill'. In this name the foreign-sounding syllables have been adapted to recognizable ones with a similar sound, much as the Italian place-name *Livorno* has become 'Leghorn' to speakers of English.

Bloomsbury is an example of a fairly late name in which a development in the meaning of the element *burh*, 'fortification', has taken place. This word is frequently found in the names of ancient fortresses, earth-works, and so on, through those of places with Norman castles, to the names of fortified manor houses, fortified towns, or just towns of any kind. *Borough* is, after all, a current legal term describing an urban settlement of a particular size and importance. In the thirteenth century it became the custom, particularly in Middlesex and Hertfordshire, to indicate by means of the termination *-bury* the central place in a great manor. The first part of these names was usually either a personal name or the name of a nearby town. Thus in Middlesex there are **Edgwarebury**—named from the adjoining place—and **Gunnersbury,** which has a personal name as its first element, as have the Hertfordshire names **Gorhambury** and **Jenningsbury** Bloomsbury was the manor of the de Blemund family, whose name in turn was derived from the French place-name, Blémont.

Careful investigation of the early forms of names avoids the pitfalls of 'obvious' meanings. If we understand that *-ham* is a frequent place-name termination, meaning 'dwelling place, manor, village', there is a great temptation to treat names like **Oakham** (R) as 'self-explanatory': 'oak village' would be an 'obvious' interpretation. But on inspection of early forms we discover *Ocham* in 1067—which at once rules out any connection with oak trees, since at that date, and for some centuries afterwards, 'oak' was still *āc*. **Oakworth** (WRY), for instance, was *Acurde* in Domesday Book (1086) and can accordingly be safely read as 'oak *worth*, i.e., oak enclosure'. The early forms of both **Oakham** and **Ockham** (Sr) point to a personal name as first element; they were, in fact, the dwelling places or manors of men sharing the same name, Oca or Occa.

In the chapters which follow, an attempt is made to study the contributions of the various inhabitants of, and visitors to, these islands to the great stock of place-names. The names of English places receive the greatest attention, it is true; but not only are these more numerous but they also show the greatest variety of types and contributing languages. The interpretations

4

offered are based on the latest information available; fortunately, place-name studies are a living and lively activity, and it is possible that new evidence will require a modification of some of the meanings given here. What will not be upset, of course, are either the general principles governing the interpreting of place-names, or the general facts about the origins and meanings of the chief elements composing the names.

2: THE COUNTIES OF ENGLAND

Apart from the 'shires' (of which there are more than twenty) the names of the various English counties can be studied in groups, according to common features in their form or meaning. Three of the northern counties, for instance, have names ending in -*land*, signifying 'tract of country'. **Northumberland** is the 'territory of the people living north of the river Humber', **Cumberland** is the 'land of the Cymry', i.e. of the Celtic people akin to those now called the Welsh, and **Westmorland** is the 'territory of the people of the western moor'. The emphasis on areas being those of particular peoples is interesting, since we normally think of one place in relation to another—south of it, or within it, for instance—whereas in earlier times human occupation of the area was more strongly stressed. As usual, the interpretation is only possible from early forms, one example of which must suffice. There is no trace of the 'people' idea in the modern name of Westmorland, but there were two additional and highly significant syllables in its tenth-century form, *Westmoringaland*, which means 'land of the Westmorings—i.e. people of the western moor'. The syllable -*ing*, still present in some modern names, will be found to convey this or similar meanings, as will be explained in Chapter 4.

The names of other counties also allude to tribes that dwelt there long ago. **Norfolk** and **Suffolk** commemorate the northern and southern peoples of the East Angles, while the East, Middle, and South Saxons are accounted for in the names of **Essex**, **Middlesex**, and **Sussex**, respectively. **Wessex**, though it designated the old West-Saxon kingdom, has never been a county name. Two county-names end in -*set* from Old English *sǣte*, 'settlers, inhabitants': **Dorset** is 'dwellers near Dorn (i.e. Dorchester)', and **Somerset**, 'dwellers near Somerton'. Both these names, it will be noticed, consist of the name of a town followed by the termination.

Kent is another name alluding to the inhabitants, being the hardly changed name of the tribe known to the Romans as the *Cantii*, 'the hosts or armies' or 'dwellers in the border

5

country'. **Devon** preserves the name of another British tribe—the *Dumnonii*, whom the Saxons called *Deofnas*. The ending of the name **Cornwall** is from OE *wealas*, 'foreigners', i.e. the British, or Welsh, as in the name **Wales** itself. The Celts of **Cornwall** called themselves *Cornovii*, or 'promontory people', and so the Saxons referred to them as *Cornwealas*—'Welsh in Kernow'; this tribal name, too, became that of a county. The name **Surrey** is partly of this type. In Old English the word was *Suther-gē*, 'southern district' i.e. of Middlesex, from which this area was settled, but it appears that the inhabitants were known as the *Suthrige*. It may well be, however, that in this case the people took their name from the place and not *vice versa*.

The counties whose names end in *-shire* extend in an unbroken block from the Lake District to the English Channel. The shape of the whole area is that of a double wedge, and it excludes all the counties so far mentioned. **Rutland** stands like a tiny island, a lone *-land* name amid the enveloping *-shires*, the discrepancy underlining its late emergence as a separate county. The ending in **Rutland** signifies merely 'estate' rather than 'tract of country', and the first part perpetuates the memory of one Rota, an early lord.

Shire (Old English *scīr*) means 'administrative division', and the first part of most of these names is the name of the county town, so that **Oxfordshire**, for instance, may be interpreted as 'administrative region centred on Oxford'—the meaning of the town name not being immediately relevant. In most of the *-shire* names the town name appears in its normal form, as in **Yorkshire**, **Worcestershire**, and **Derbyshire**, but in some there is a slight modification. **Lancashire**, for instance, is the shire of **Lancaster**, and **Cheshire**, that of **Chester**. The connection between **Shropshire** and its county town is not so clear until we note that the early form of **Shrewsbury** was *Scrobbesbyrig* (pronounced 'Shrobbesburi'), the county being called *Scrobbesbyrigscir* in the eleventh century. The *byrig* soon dropped out of the county name, which then approached its modern form. The Normans found both town and county names hard to pronounce, and turned them into *Salopesberia* and *Salopescira*, from which is derived the abbreviation Salop, now the official name of the reorganised county.

Hampshire is another county name in which it is difficult at first to observe the name of the town concerned. **Southampton** was formerly called *Hampton*—*South* being added later to distinguish it from the Midland county-town, **Northampton**. Despite the similarity of their later forms, the two Hamptons had different origins; Northampton was from *hām-tūn*, 'home farm', but Southampton was from *hamm-tūn*, 'farmstead on level land beside a river'. *Hamtunscir* in course of time became *Hantescir*—whence the abbreviation 'Hants.'

The county-town names are of various origins. One *-shire* name (**Derby**), is Scandinavian, many of the others Old English, and some have a history stretching back to Romano-British times. Explanations of these names will be found in later chapters. **Berkshire** is the only *-shire* name which does not contain the name of its county town. The first element here is the name of a district, *Berroc*, said to have been a forest, but in turn named after a hill, since it seems to be related to the British word, *barro*, 'top or summit'.

The only county now remaining to be mentioned is **Durham**. This name is unique in England, being shared in its simple form by both county and town. Originally *Dunholm*—a Scandinavian word meaning 'hill island'—the name was modified to something like its modern form by the Normans. Their *Durelme* or *Dureaume* was given a more English appearance by the *-ham* spelling adopted in recent centuries.

The two largest shires were each subdivided into three areas, which later became administrative counties. The Yorkshire **Ridings**—East, **West,** and **North**—are the 'third parts' of the shire, the Scandinavian *thrithjung*, from which their names are derived, being used in this sense in Norway and Iceland. The initial *Th-* in time attached itself to the preceding word, so that *North Thrithjun*g became **North Riding**, and so on. Each section of Lincolnshire is called 'parts', to which is added a distinctive name. **Lindsey** (or Parts of **Lindsey**) means 'Lindon island', *Lindon* being the old name for the city of Lincoln. The area was originally surrounded by water. **Kesteven** is a mixed name, comprising Celtic and Scandinavian elements. The first part is the British word meaning 'wooded area'; the second is a Scandinavian expression meaning 'meeting place or administrative district'. **Holland** is of English origin, and means 'land by a spur of a hill'. Lindsey is still further subdivided—into **North, West,** and **South Ridings.**

As a result of local government reorganisation there have been changes in nomenclature. Some names, e.g. Rutland, Huntingdon, Westmorland, have disappeared from the list of counties. New names include adaptations of river-names and existing county-names prefixed by North, South, East, or West.

3: BRITONS AND ROMANS

When the Romans arrived in Britain, these islands were inhabited by numerous tribes, usually independent, but sometimes bound in loose alliances, and frequently at war among themselves. Most of these people were Celts, though there were undoubtedly also some representatives of an earlier population. Even the Celts were not a homogeneous people, having come in successive waves from different parts of Continental Europe, and their diversity showed itself—among other ways—in differences of language. Some were speakers of Brythonic (or Brittonic) dialects, from which modern Welsh and Breton are derived; the other group are known as Goidelic, represented today by the Gaelic of Scotland, Ireland, and the Isle of Man.

The earliest records of British place-names date from the centuries of the Roman occupation. Documents mentioning these names were either in Greek or in Latin, and so the exact form of the name often remains slightly uncertain, owing to the addition of classical terminations to the Celtic word-stems. Much work on the early languages of Britain has, however, been done during the past forty or fifty years, and it is now possible to offer interpretations of many names that were regarded as obscure in the early years of this century.

It is not surprising that in England there are to be found fewer names of Celtic origin than in Wales, say, or in Scotland, but the number of such names (as well as the importance of some of the places concerned) is quite substantial.

London, for instance, was *Londinium* in the Latin records, interpreted as 'town of Londinos'—the personal name meaning 'wild'. **Reculver** (K) was *Regulbium*—'headland'; **Penkridge** (St) similarly shows but little change from its original form, *Pennocrucium*, which means 'summit of a mound'. **Pentridge** (Do) is also thought to contain the same two elements (*penno*, 'summit', and *cruc*, 'mound'), though the second syllable here may be from a word meaning 'boar'.

Dover (K), as *Dubris*, was mentioned as early as A.D. 4. The British word means 'waters', i.e. 'the stream', and refers to the river Dour, and not to the English Channel. **Wendover** (Bk) also contains this element and means 'white waters', appropriately describing the clear chalk stream there. Other names surviving almost unchanged from Celtic originals include **Eccles** (La), 'church', **Lympne** (K), 'elm place', and **Catterick** (NRY), which means 'waterfall'.

Lincoln was originally *Lindon*, though *Colonia*, 'colony', was added at some time during the Roman occupation. The modern name combines the two elements, the first of which means 'pool'. **Carlisle** (Cu) also contains an early Celtic name to which another word has been prefixed. *Luguvallium* (the earliest form of the name, dating from A.D. 4) is interpreted as 'Luguvalos's place'; a connection with the war-god, Lugus, has also been suggested, though it may well be that the British leader Luguvalos was a devoted follower of the god. *Caer*, meaning 'fort', was not added until the eleventh century. This usage is found in modern Welsh forms of English place-names, e.g. *Cair Ebrauc* for York, or *Cair Wysg* for Exeter.

York is a particularly interesting name. The Celtic *Eboracum* is derived from the personal name Eburos, presumably that of the first settler or an early ruler, which is itself connected with a word meaning 'yew tree'. The contraction *Ebor.*, it is of interest to note, is used as part of the signature of the Archbishop of York. The British name was changed to *Eoforwic* ('boar farm') by the early English settlers (in much the same way that Ypres became 'Wipers' to British warriors a millennium and a half later), and succeeding invaders—the Danes—modified the name to suit their tongues, calling the place *Iorvik*. *Yeork*, and then *York*, developed from this last form by the thirteenth century. This name can therefore claim to be Celtic in origin, but it is surely unique in the way its development so concisely records the history of early England.

Leeds has undergone merely a vowel change from its Celtic original, *Loidis*. The name was originally applied to the whole district around the modern city and is usually explained as 'district on the river'.

A fairly numerous class of names comprises those with a Celtic stem to which has been added a suffix of English (or other) origin. Under this heading come the *-chester* names, about which a few misconceptions can perhaps be removed. First, it must be emphasised that although a majority of names with the termination *-chester* (or *-ceter*, *-cester*, *-caster*, etc.) refer to places that were formerly Roman military stations or towns, this ending does not represent the Latin word *castra*, 'camp', applied to the place by the Romans. The Old English word *ceaster*, though undoubtedly derived from *castra*, is the immediate source in all these names, and was used to mean 'city' or (less frequently) 'fortified place'. Secondly, and following the usual rule of place-name interpretation, it must not be assumed that every modern name ending in *-chester* belongs to this class. At least one well-known name—Grantchester (C)—has a completely different origin, as will be explained in the next chapter.

A number of places bear the British town-name together with the termination. These include **Manchester** (*Mamucio*—'breast-shaped hill'), **Gloucester** (*Glevum*—'bright place'), and **Worcester**—('chief town of the Wigoran tribe'). **Winchester** (Ha) contains the old name *Venta*, 'market'. The meaning of *Viroconium*, now **Wroxeter** (Sa), is unknown. **Chester,** besides being called *Deva*, was also known as *Civitas Legionum* ('city of the legions'); this, it has been pointed out, must have been early

9

abbreviated to *Legionum*, to produce the Old English *Legaceaster*. By the eleventh century this, too, had been shortened to *Ceaster*, perhaps because of confusion with the then current name of **Leicester** which was *Ligoraceaster* in 942. **Chester** was regarded as of sufficient importance to forgo the distinctive prefix, but **Leicester** was felt to require its label 'of the Ligoran people'.

Other *-chester* names of Celtic origin consist of a British river-name followed by this suffix. **Exeter** (D) is a notable example; this is 'town on the Exe', the river being originally *Isca*—'water'. **Lancaster** (La) is named from the river Lune (*Loin*—'health-giving'). **Frocester** (Gl) is on the river Frome ('brisk one'), but no meaning can be assigned to the name of the river—the Colne—on which **Colchester** (E) stands, and it has even been suggested that this river-name was taken over by the Celts from an earlier people.

Salisbury (W) and **Lichfield** (St) are rare examples of names consisting of a Celtic root to which is added an English suffix other than *-ceaster*. *Sorviodunum*, the British name for Salisbury, has to be interpreted merely as 'Sorbio fort', since the meaning of the first element is unknown. The Saxons translated the second component by their word *burh*, producing the Old English *Searobyrg;* this in turn suffered at the hands (or in the mouths) of the Normans, who duly transformed it to *Salesbiri* by the thirteenth century. **Lichfield** has a forest name as its first element; the British name *Letocetum* means 'grey wood', and the early English form *Liccidfeld* adopts the Celtic term quite faithfully, with the addition of *feld* 'open land'.

Many names in Cornwall are of Celtic origin, including those of the larger towns. **Bodmin**, 'house of the monks', reminds us that there was a monastery there, said to have been founded by King Athelstan in 926. **Penzance** also has religious associations, being 'holy headland', from the central position of the church on its shore. **Mevagissey** is '(church of) St Mew and St Ida', celebrating, like other names of the peninsula, the numerous saints who flourished there in the Dark Ages. Other names relate to geographical features: **Camborne** is 'crooked hill', **Looe**, 'inlet of the sea', and **Redruth**, 'red ford'. **Penwith**, the old name for Land's End, means 'promontory seen from afar'. Several names commencing with *Perran-* commemorate St Peran: **Perranar-worthal** is 'St Peran in the marshes,' **Perranporth** is 'St Peran's port', and **Perranzabuloe**, 'St Peran in the sand'—the termination here being the Latin *in sabulo*. **Fowey** is 'beech river', and **Marazion**, 'little market'.

Many river-names are Celtic, though they have usually to be rather disappointingly translated as 'stream' or 'water'. These

10

include **Wear, Don** and **Avon,** as well as names derived from British *Isca*—'water': **Axe, Exe, Esk, Usk,** and **Wiske. Ouse** has a similar general meaning, as have **Dore, Wey** and **Wye. Thames, Thame,** and **Tame** constitute another group, all meaning 'dark'. **Test** means 'strong running'. **Trent** and **Tarrant** are related and mean 'trespasser', suggesting their liability to flooding. **Dee** is the 'holy one', **Taw** 'silent one', and **Dove** 'dark one'. **Derwent** and **Darwen** contain the element *derua* 'oak'; **Leam, Lymn,** and **Leven** are from a word meaning 'elm'.

This survey of names of Celtic origin is necessarily incomplete, and takes no account of the many names introduced during and after the Old English period, particularly on the Welsh Border and in the north-west of England.

4: GERMANIC INVADERS

After numerous raiding expeditions over a long period of time, invaders from across the North Sea began to settle in Britain in the fifth century A.D. It is all too easy to think of the Anglo-Saxon settlement as something like a modern invasion; instead, we should do better to imagine a slowed-down version of the settlement of North America. As the colonists spread westwards, they either founded new settlements or established themselves in British villages. As more and more invaders came, and as the population grew, more and more land needed to be prepared for cultivation—often by the clearance of extensive forests. The progress of this settlement is recorded, at least in part, in place-names.

It is possible that the earliest English (i.e. Anglo-Saxon) place-names are those of a special type, viz., those with a personal name as their first element and with the termination *-ingas* affixed. These names were originally applied to tribes, or rather folk; the bearers of the name were the followers or dependants of the man concerned, but were not necessarily related by blood. The followers of one Hæsta, for instance, were the *Hæstingas*, and their settlement has become the modern **Hastings. Havering** was the settlement of the *Hæferingas*—'Hæfer's people'; **Barling** (E) that of 'Bærla's people'; **Worthing** (Sx) the settlement of the *Wurthingas*—'Wurth's people'. Other examples are **Braughing** (Hrt), **Reading** (Brk), **Elsing** (Nf), and **Cooling** (K). It will be noticed that most of these names now end in *-ing*, not *-ings*.

An early development of these names was the addition of the element *-hām*, 'homestead, settlement', indicating a transition from a folk-name to a place-name properly so called. **Billingham**

11

(Du), **Messingham** (L), and **Nottingham** belong to this class, respectively the settlements of the people of Billa, Mæssa, and Snot. The initial *s* is lost in the modern **Nottingham,** but retained in **Snainton** (Nt), which contains the same personal name (Snot). Norman scribes were responsible for the mutilation, though curiously the shorter name has regained its lost initial. **Birmingham** also belongs here—'homestead of Beorma's people'. An interesting set of names is to be found in Surrey and Berkshire, viz. **Woking** (Sr), **Wokingham** (Brk), and **Wokefield** (Brk). All refer to a certain Wocc, the last being his (or his people's) 'open land'.

Other evidence of early formation is provided by archaic words used in place-names. The element *-gē*, 'district' has already been mentioned in the discussion of **Surrey** in Chapter 2. This same ancient term is found in **Ely** (C) 'Eel district', **Vange** (E) 'Fen district', and **Lyminge** (K) 'district by the river Limen'. Another obsolete term is *ēar* 'mud', which occurs in **Erith** (K) *Ēar-hyth*, 'muddy landing-place'.

Names referring to pagan religion are also regarded as particularly early. This is a reasonable inference, especially when one remembers the energy with which the early converts destroyed pagan shrines and other evidence of their previous faith. Divinities are commemorated in **Wednesbury** (St), **Tysoe** (Wa), and **Thursley** (Sr)—places sacred to Woden, Tiw, and Thunor. Less certainly ancient are names relating to dragons, ogres, spectres, etc. **Shuckburgh** (Wa) is 'demon's hill'; **Drakelow** (Db) is 'dragon's mound'; **Pook's Hill** (Sx) is 'hill haunted by a goblin'. Heathen temples are referred to in **Harrow** (Mx), **Pepper Harrow** (Sx), and **Arrowfield** (Wo)—all derived from OE *hearg*, 'temple'; from *wēoh* or *wīg*, of the same meaning, are derived **Weedon** (Nth), **Winwood** (Hrt), and **Patchway** (Sx)—the last being 'Pæcca's temple'.

Before passing to a consideration of some common elements in names of Old English origin, an explanation must now be offered of some county-town names not discussed in Chapter 2. **Hereford** is probably 'army ford', suggesting that the crossing was both wide and important. Several other county towns were sited on fords. **Stafford** was 'ford by a landing place'; **Oxford** 'ford for oxen'; **Bedford,** 'Beda's ford'; and **Hertford** 'stag ford'. **Buckingham** has a final element *hamm*, 'enclosure, ground by a river', the land being that of Bucc's people. **Cambridge** has developed interestingly from OE *Grantebrycg*, though earlier it was *Grantacaestir*, which invited comparison with **Grantchester**. The latter, as pointed out in Chapter 3, is not a *ceaster* name at all, though clearly **Cambridge** once was! The old name meant 'bridge over the river Granta', and both river- and town-names have been similarly transformed. **Grantchester** ('settlers on the Granta') preserves the former river-name, to which has been added *sǣte*, 'settlers'.

Huntingdon is 'huntsman's hill'. **Warwick** has as its second element the common term *wīc*, which is perhaps best rendered by a general word such as 'premises'. The element is found in a wide variety of names. The most satisfactory equivalent of **Warwick** seems to be 'premises of the dwellers by the weir'.

The element *wīc* is one of the most common in place-names of Old English origin. It is attached, for instance, to words indicating direction, e.g. **Northwich** (Ch), **Southwick** (Sx), **Eastwick** (WRY), and **Westwick** (WRY). **Norwich** (Nf) also belongs to this group. Sometimes the main element is a word referring to a tree or other plant, as in **Ashwick** (So), **Hazelwick** (Sx), **Slaughterwicks** (Sr—from *slāh-trēow*, 'sloe-tree'), **Bromwich** (Wa 'broom'), and **Rushwick** (Wo). A fairly large number of *-wīc* names refer to dairy products, probably giving rise to the frequent interpretation 'dairy farm'. **Butterwick** is found in several counties including Durham, Lancashire, and Westmorland; **Cheswick** (Nb), **Chiswick** (C, E, Mx), **Keswick** (Cu) all relate to cheese. Other products include wool (**Woolwich**, K), salt (**Saltwick**, Nb), and honey (**Honeywick**, Sx).

Another termination that is found in many names of Anglo-Saxon origin is *-worth*—'enclosure'. The simple form is found in **Worth** (Sx, K, Do, Ch). **Highworth** (W) and **Littleworth** (Brk) are self-explanatory, as are **Longworth** (La), **Clayworth** (Nt), **Thistleworth** (Sx), and **Duckworth** (La). **Minsterworth** (Gl) was a possession of St Peter's monastery, Gloucester, **Hinxworth** (Hrt) was 'horse enclosure'; **Lindworth** (Wo) alludes to lime trees, **Turnworth** (Do) to thorn trees. Sometimes the ending is disguised, as in **Abinger** (Sr)—'enclosure of the people of Eabba', **Plumford** (K)—'plum enclosure', **Cotchford** (Sx—'thicket enclosure', and **Clarewood** (Nb)—'clover enclosure'. The most common type of *-worth* name, however, has an Old English personal name as the first element. Examples are **Isleworth** (Mx) (Gislere), **Wandsworth** (Sr—now Greater London) (Wendel), **Rickmansworth** (Hrt) (Ricmær), and **Ashmansworth** (Ha) (Æscmær). Related terminations, with the same meaning, are *-worthy*, frequently found in Devon and Cornwall, and *-wardine* (OE *worthign*), common in the West Midlands. Examples of the first are **Fernworthy, Thornworthy, Highworthy, Langworthy,** and **Smallworthy**—all in Devon, and all self-explanatory. **Canworthy** (Co) is 'enclosure with a cairn'; **Curworthy** (D) is 'mill enclosure'. Formations with personal names are very common. The following examples are all in Devon: **Woolfardisworthy** (Wulfheard) has the distinction of being the longest single-word place-name in England; **Hamsworthy** (Heremōd), **Blatchworthy** (Blacci), **Natsworthy** (Hnott), and **Wilsworthy** (Wifel) all include Old English personal names; **Derworthy** and **Stroxworthy** have post-Norman Conquest names as their first element, showing that *worthy* was still very much alive at the end of the Anglo-Saxon period.

The West Midland *-wardine* is also found further afield, e.g in **Worden** and **Worthen** (D). **Cheswardine** (Sa) is 'cheese enclosure'; **Stanwardine** (Sa) is 'stone enclosure'. **Ellardine** (Sa), **Ingardine** (Sa), **Pedwardine** (He), and **Tollardine** (Wo) all have personal names as their first element.

By far the commonest Old English element, however, is *tūn*— 'enclosure, farmstead, village'. Unlike *worth*, this element never occurs alone, and is very rare as a first element—**Tonbridge** (K) being a possible case, though it has been suggested that the first syllable here is from a personal name, *Tunna*. Very common indeed are *-tūn* names indicating location in relation to other places, e.g. the many instances of **Norton, Sutton, Weston,** and **Easton, Aston,** or **Eston.** This is good evidence that these are not the earliest names in the locality; **Sutton Coldfield** is named as south of (and therefore junior to) **Lichfield; Kings Norton** is north of (and therefore established later than) **Bromsgrove.** Villages may be above others—hence the many examples of **Upton**—or below them, and so **Nareton** (K). Villages may be old or new, attractive in summer or tolerable in winter, noteworthy as possessing a church or a mill, or famous for a product: **Alton** (Bd), **Naunton** (Gl) and **Newtown** (Gl, Ha, Nb, Wt), **Somerton** (L, Nf, O, So), **Winterton** (Nf), **Cheriton** (D), **Millington** (Ch), **Butterton** (St), **Honington** (Wa) and **Honiton** (D).

Some names ending in *-tūn* allude to nearby natural features, such as a brook, in **Brockton** (Sa), **Brotton** (NRY), and **Broughton** (Bk, Cu, Db, La), a marsh, as in the frequent names **Marston** and **Merston,** or a wood, as in the equally common **Wotton** and **Wootton.** Domestic and wild animals, and cultivated and wild plants are referred to in **Calverton** (Nt), **Lambton** (Nb), **Oxton** (Ch), **Shepton** (So), **Skipton** (NRY), **Foxton** (Lei), **Flaxton** (NRY), **Linton** (He), **Ryton** (Du), **Brereton** (St), **Nettleton** (L), **Rushton** (Ch), and **Lemmington** (Nb)—the last-named commemorating the speedwell, *hleomuc* in Old English. Many other names are self-explanatory, e.g. **Aston, Appleton, Elmton** (Db), **Plumpton** (Cu), **Thornton.** Some names allude to tribes living outside their usual area: **Exton** (Ha) was the home of East Saxons in Wessex, **Saxton** (C) that of some Saxons in Anglian territory. Some at least of the **Walton** names belong here— derived from OE *walh*, 'foreigner'. Some late examples of the form include post-Conquest personal names, even surnames:

Bryanston (Do) perpetuates the memory of Brian de Insula, who flourished in the early thirteenth century; **Cripstone** (Co) commemorates Henry Cryspyn (1356); **Flamston** (W) has as its first element the name of Walter Flambard (1202).

Another fairly common element is found in **Aldenham** (Hrt), **Newnham** (Gl), **Northam** (D), **Southam** (Gl), **Eastham** (Ch), and **Westerham** (K). These are compounds of *hām*, 'a village, community, manor, or homestead', the first elements here being 'old', 'new', 'north', 'south', 'east', and 'west'. The nature of the soil is alluded to in **Chartham** (K), 'rocky village', **Greatham** (Du) and **Greetham** (L), 'village on gravel', and **Flintham** (Nt). **Faversham** (K), **Garboldisham** (Nf), **Saxmundham** (Sf), **Offham** (K), **Pagham** (Sx), **Fakenham** (Nf), and **Meopham** (K) all contain personal names; **Babraham** (C) has as its first element the woman's name Beaduburg. The compound form *hām-stede* is regarded as a unit in many names, e.g. **Hampstead** (Mx, Brk), with its variants **Hamstead** (St, Wt) and **Hempstead** (E, Nf). This name, usually rendered 'homestead, farm', is frequently found with the name of a tree or other plant as the first element, as **Ashampstead** (Brk), **Nettlestead** (K), **Nuthampstead** and **Wheathampstead** (Hrt), all of which require no further explanation. **Berkhamsted** (Hrt) possibly alludes to birch trees, **Palmstead** (K) to the pear; **Easthampstead** (Brk) is shown by its early forms (e.g. *Yethamstede*, 1176) to be the 'homestead by the gate'—possibly the gate to Windsor Forest. **Hemel Hempstead** (Hrt) is 'homestead in Hamel, i.e. broken country'; the district-name, Hamel, was incorporated in some early forms and *Hem-lampsted* produced the modern spelling *Hem-*. *Hemel* was then reintroduced as a separate word. Another development from *hām* was *hām-tūn*, also regarded as a unitary element, meaning 'home farm'. The compounds are often self-explanatory, e.g. **Littlehampton** (Sx), **Netherhampton** (W), **Northampton** (Nth), and **Oakhampton** (Wo). Note that **Southampton** (Ha) is not among these names, being more probably a compound of *hamm* 'enclosure, water-meadow'; neither is **Okehampton** (D), which was *Ocmundtun*, 'village on river Okement'.

The termination *-ley* in modern names is often from OE *lēah*, which presents a number of difficulties in interpreting. Its primary meaning was 'wood, clearing in a wood'. The element occurs alone in a number of names such as **Lea** (L), **Lee** (Bk, E, Ha, K, Sa), **Leigh** (Brk, Ch, D, Gl, Ha, K, So, Sr, W), **Leese** (Ch), and **Leam** (Du, Nb). The common **Bradley** is 'broad clearing'; **Henley** (O), **Langley** (frequent), and **Rowley** (D, Du, St, WRY) are clearings which are 'high', 'long', and 'rough', respectively. Tree-names are also frequently found; the oak is alluded to in **Acklam** (ERY, NRY), **Acle** (Nf), **Eagle** (L), **Oak-**

leigh (K), **Oakley** (Bd, Bk, Wo), and **Ocle** (He). The birch contributes to **Berkeley** (Gl) and **Berkley** (So). **Ashley** (Bk, C, Ch, D), **Boxley** (K), **Elmley** (Wo), and **Thornley** (Du) are self-explanatory. **Lindley** (WRY) refers to the lime, **Uley** (Gl) to the yew, and **Weedley** (ERY), **Withiel** (So), and **Willey** (Ch, He, Sa, Wa) all allude to the willow. Animal names occur in **Brockley** (So) 'badger', **Foxley** (He), **Hartley** (Do, K, So), **Woolley** (Brk, Hu, WRY) 'wolf', **Oxley** (St), **Shepley** (WRY), **Shipley** (Db), 'sheep', **Horseley** (Db), **Cowley** (Gl), and **Lambley** (Nt).

Fortification was important in the days when territory and survival were almost synonymous, and so it is not surprising that there should be references in place-names to fortified places. The Old English word *burh* was applied to earth-works and camps of what is now designated the prehistoric period, to former Roman camps and stations, and to Anglo-Saxon defensive works. Ancient encampments are found at **Cadbury** (So), **Cholesbury** (Bk), **Badbury** (Do), and **Woodborough** (Nt). Roman stations are alluded to in **Brough** (Nt, ERY, NRY) and **Richborough** (K)—the old name *Rutupiæ* constituting the first syllable of the latter name. **Hertingfordbury** (Hrt) is an instance of Anglo-Saxon fortification; this name was *Hertfordingburi*—'fort of the *Hertfordings*, i.e. people of Hertford'. In later names, the termination merely signifies 'fortified manor house', and even 'manor'; examples are **Prestbury** (Ch) and **Bassettbury** (Bk). Middlesex (now Greater London) names include **Bloomsbury**, **Edgewarebury** and **Gunnersbury**. In **Newbury** (Brk), the word has the sense of 'chartered borough'. The usual compass points and plant names are to be found as first elements in **Sudbury** (Sf), **Norbury** (Ch, Db, Sa, Sr), **Westbury** (Bk, Gl), **Eastbury** (Brk), **Flexbury** (Co), **Thornbury** (He) and **Thornborough** (Nb, WRY).

Modern names ending in *-borough* may originate in OE *beorg*, 'hill, mound'. **Farnborough** (Brk, Ha, K) is 'fern-covered hill'; **Whatborough** (Lei) is 'wheat hill'; **Hillborough** (K) is not so repetitive as it looks, as the first element was once *halig*, 'holy'. **Woodnesborough** (K) seems to have been a mound sacred to the god Woden, and the hill at **Modbury** (Do) appears to have been used for the *mōt* or assembly.

This rapid survey of a few of the most common place-name elements of Anglo-Saxon origin has only scratched the surface of the whole body of names dating from between 500 and 900 A.D. The process of naming by no means stopped at the second of those dates, however, and the next chapter will show that new waves of invaders played their own part in assigning, modifying, or replacing names in the places where they settled.

5: NORSEMEN AND NORMANS

The last quarter of the ninth century saw extensive Scandinavian settlement in the north and east of England. A separate wave of invaders came a little later to north-west England—not direct from their northern homeland, but from Ireland, where there had been Scandinavian colonies for about a century. The earlier settlers (those on the east) were mostly Danes; those from Ireland were of Norwegian origin, evidently still speaking their native language, but markedly influenced by the Irish.

The Scandinavian colonisation was neither so prolonged nor so widespread as the Anglo-Saxon settlement, and so there are relatively few place-names to bear witness to it. Moreover these names are restricted to the 'Danelaw' (i.e., the area to the north and east of Watling Street—roughly a line from London to Chester). Within the Danelaw, the distribution of Scandinavian names is uneven, with heavy concentrations in the North and East Ridings of Yorkshire, the Lake District, Cheshire, Lincolnshire, the East Midlands, and East Anglia.

The most common termination of Scandinavian names in England is -*by*, usually rendered by 'village'—with good reason, since most of the places concerned were established before the Vikings took them over. If it is realised that the process was essentially one of *re-naming*, some of the peculiarities of the names ending in -*by* will be better understood. One of these peculiarities is that the termination is quite often added to an Old English word, e.g. **Utterby** (L), in which the first element is OE *uterra*, 'outer, more remote'; there is another Lincolnshire place, **Itterby,** in which the first element is the corresponding ON word, *ytri*. It is likely, of course, that what was felt to be a foreign element was eventually replaced by a word from the vernacular, as is almost certain to have happened in names like **Newby** (Cu). The frequent **Asby** shows a replacement of ON *askr* by OE *æsc*. In **Asby** (We) the Scandinavian form remains undisturbed. **Selby** (WRY) is 'village with willows'; **Linby** (Nt) is 'village with lime trees'; **Thrimby** (We) is 'thorn-bush village'. **Derby** is of interest for several reasons. One is that it belongs to the rare group of county-town names of Scandinavian origin; another is that this is known to be a complete replacement of an English name—*Northworthy*. The Scandinavian name means 'village with a deer park'. **Kirkby** or **Kirby,** 'village with a church', is very common in the Danelaw, as also is **Crosby,** 'village with a cross'. **Coningsby** and **Conisby** (L) seem to have been owned by a king (ON *kunung*), and **Whenby** (NRY) by women.

17

This ending is frequently added to personal names; these may be Scandinavian, as in **Brumby** (L), **Raceby** (Du), **Oadby** (Lei) and **Stainsby** (Db), Irish, as in **Duggleby** (ERY) and **Lackenby** (NRY), English, as in **Audleby** (L), **Ellerby** (NRY), and **Gutterby** (Cu), or even Norman, as in the Cumberland names **Allonby**, **Harraby**, and **Ponsonby**. **Grimsby** (L), which contains the Scandinavian name Grim, is probably the best-known example of this group.

Whitby (NRY), 'white village', is another replacement name, having been preceded by OE *Streonæshalch* ('Streon's nook') and then by ON *Prestby* ('priests' village'). Lastly, and omitting many examples (there are 150 names ending in -*by* in the North Riding alone), a word must be said on names like **Danby** (NRY). Meaning 'village of the Danes', this name indicates a Danish settlement in an area predominantly occupied by another people; their neighbours may in fact have been English, and the use of such a name points to the existence of a living Anglo-Scandinavian dialect in the area concerned. Similar names are **Normanby** (L, NRY), 'Norwegians' village', **Firseby** (L), **Frisby** (Lei), 'Frisians' village', and **Ingleby** (Db, L, NRY), 'village of the English'.

The element *thorp* is also a very common one in Scandinavian names. Meaning 'secondary settlement' it is often used together with the name of the parent village, e.g. **Barkby Thorpe** (Lei), **Tattershall Thorpe** (L), **Scotton Thorpe** (WRY), and **Welwick Thorpe** (ERY). When compass names are used, they indicate the position of the daughter settlement relative to the original village, e.g. **Easthorpe** and **Westhorpe** (Nt), dependencies of Southwell, east and west of it respectively. **Littlethorpe** (WRY), **Newthorpe** (Nt, WRY), **Woodthorpe** (WRY), **Milnthorpe** (Nt, We, WRY), and **Bishopthorpe** (WRY) are all formed from Old English bases (and are all self-explanatory), whereas **Coneysthorpe** (NRY) and **Skinnerthorpe** (WRY) have as their first element ON *kunung*, 'king' and *skinnari*, 'skinner'.

Thorp is combined very frequently with Old Norse personal names, as in **Alethorpe** (Nf), **Caythorpe** (ERY), **Grimethorpe** (WRY), **Kettlethorpe** (WRY), and **Sibthorpe** (Nt). **Streetthorpe** (WRY) has no connection with a Roman road (the usual meaning of names containing *Street-*, *Strat-*, or *Stret-*) but is derived from the ON personal name Styr; **Oakthorpe** (Lei) is also deceptive, being from ON Aki; **Bromkinsthorpe** (Lei)—*Bruneskinnestorp* in 1233—has as first element the Scandinavian nickname *Brun-skinn*, 'one with brown skin'. This element evidently continued in use after the Norman Conquest, witness such names as **Countesthorpe** (Lei), or **Donisthorpe** (Lei), which contains the Old French personal name Durand, or

Painsthorpe (ERY)—which has as first element the Middle English surname Pain.

The meanings 'clearing in a forest, meadow, paddock' are assigned to *thwaite*, another very common element in names of Scandinavian origin. There may be prefixed to this adjectives relating to size, shape, etc. as in **Braithwaite** (Cu), 'broad clearing', **Micklethwaite** (Cu, WRY) 'great clearing', **Langthwaite** (Cu, La, NRY) 'long clearing', and **Smaithwaite** (Cu) 'small clearing'. Tree-names occur in **Applethwaite** (Cu), **Hawthornthwaite** (La), **Thornthwaite** (Cu, We, WRY), and **Birthwaite** (WRY)—the last alluding to the birch tree; names of plants, wild and cultivated are found in **Brackenthwaite** (Cu, WRY), **Beanthwaite** (La) and **Bruthwaite** (Cu—'briar clearing'). Less easy to identify are **Slaithwaite** (WRY), 'sloe clearing', **Thackthwaite** (NRY, Cu), 'clearing where thatching material was obtained', **Seathwaite** (Cu), 'sedge clearing', and **Haverthwaite** (La) and **Linethwaite** (Cu), 'oats clearing' and 'flax clearing', respectively. More than ten per cent of first elements consist of personal names, as in **Austhwaite** (Cu), **Gunnerthwaite** (La), **Hampsthwaite** (WRY), **Outhwaite** (La), and **Wickerthwaite** (Cu).

There are many names of mixed origin, but there is room for only a small selection here. Apart from the replacement of a complete OE name by one of Scandinavian origin, as we have seen in connection with **Derby** and **Whitby**, there occurred also the replacement of an English personal name by a Norse one, while retaining the OE ending (e.g. *-tūn*), as in **Gonalston** (Nt), **Keddleston** (Db), and the Leicestershire names of **Thurcaston**, **Thurlaston**, and **Thurmaston**, which contain respectively the Norse personal names Thorketil, Thorleif, and Thormod. There are so many examples of **Grimston** (Lei, Nf, Nt, Sf, ERY, NRY)— together with the fact that Grim is such a frequent Norse personal name—that these mixed names are often called 'Grimston hybrids'. Sometimes the first element was an OE common noun, as in **Stainley** (WRY), in which OE *stān* has given way to the corresponding ON *steinn*, 'stone'. In **Rawcliffe** (NRY), 'red cliff', OE *rēad* has been replaced by ON *rauthr;* the usual development of *Readeclife*, which is an actual early form of this name, is **Radcliffe** (La, Lei, Mx, Nt) or **Redcliff** (So). The second element has been replaced in **Beckwith** (WRY), **Rudston** (ERY), and **Badby** (Nth); the early forms for these were *Becwudu*, 'beech wood', *Rodstan*, 'rood stone', and *Baddanbyrig*, 'Badda's fort'.

The Scandinavian way of life is commemorated in many place-names. Social, political, and legal organization can be detected in names like **Yarlside** (La), '*jarl*'s shieling (mountain pasture)', **Holderness** (ERY), '*hold*'s promontory', and **Dringhoe** (ERY), '*dreng*'s mound', which allude to three orders in Viking society: the *jarl*, or nobleman, the *hold*, or yeoman, and the *dreng*, or free tenant. The *bondi* ('free landowner') is alluded to in **Bonby** (L), and the *leysung* ('freedman') in **Lazenby** (NRY). The ON term for a third part, *thrithjung*, has a technical application in the division of territories, such as counties. The **East, West,** and **North Ridings** of Yorkshire, and the **North, South,** and **West Ridings** of the Parts of Lindsey in Lincolnshire are derived from the term; misdivision of *North thrithjung*, etc., brought about *North-rithjung*, etc., and so arose the modern forms of these names. Scandinavian public assemblies are alluded to in **Fingay Hill** (NRY)—*thing-haugr*, 'assembly mound'—and the former name of **Hanger Hill** (Nt), *Thinghowe*. The Tynwald, or Isle of Man parliament, is so called from the Scandinavian custom of holding such assemblies in an appointed field, known as *thing-vollr*, which is the origin also of **Thingwall** (Ch, La) and, in Scotland, of **Dingwall** (Ross).

The Scandinavians of the north-west of the country brought with them from Ireland certain linguistic features which appear in the place-names of the area, such as the word *erg*, 'shieling', borrowed from Old Irish, found in **Arrowe** (Ch), **Arras** (ERY), **Eryholme** (NRY), **Argam** (ERY), and **Arram** (ERY). The term *shieling* seems to have been applied not only to the mountain pastures used in summer, but also to the huts which the herdsmen occupied throughout the season. Such shelters could be constructed of turf—hence **Torver** (La), brushwood—as in **Tirril** (We), or stout poles (*stafn*), alluded to in **Stephney** (Cu). They might be situated on a precipice (ON *bjarg*), as **Berrier** (Cu) evidently was; near a mossy bog, like **Mosser** (Cu) and **Mozergh** (We); in the middle, as was **Medlar** (La); or in a windy, exposed position, e.g. **Winder** (La, We). Very often the first element is an ON or OIr personal name, as in **Anglesark** (La), **Battrix** (WRY), **Mansergh** (We), and **Goosnargh** (La). Lastly, mention must be made of 'inversion compounds', also a feature of the naming by these colonists of the north-west. Personal names normally occur as the first element in compounds, as has already been seen in many instances. In a number of names in this area, however, the Celtic pattern is followed, and the personal name comes second. Examples are **Kirkandrews** (Cu) (three examples), **Kirkoswald** (Cu), **Aspatria** (Cu)—'Patrick's ash', and **Seat Sandal** (We)—'Sandolf's shieling'.

It was not only the British Isles that received the attentions of the Vikings; among other places, Northern France was also raided by them, and subsequently colonised. The province on which they concentrated received, as a result, the name *Normandy*. The Norman Conquest of England was, therefore, yet another incursion of Northmen. In the meantime, the Norse language had ceased to be the vernacular of these men, and when they came to this country they were speaking a dialect of French, stubbornly refusing even to be able to pronounce the tongue of their grandfathers; the name of King Cnut, for instance, became *Canute* to the Normans, and place-names underwent a similar mutilation. Initial *s* was a difficulty to them: **Tutbury** (St) has been maimed in this way, being 'Stut's fortress'; **Nottingham,** as we have already seen, is what the Normans made of *Snotinga-ham*. Clusters of consonants were difficult to them, hence the modern **Durham** from the early form *Dunholm*, by way of *Durelme* and *Dureaume*. **Cambridge** developed from *Grantebrige* because this latter form presented pronunciation problems to the Normans. In many instances, however, the alterations were temporary, and modern forms of the names concerned resemble their OE progenitors more closely than they do the Domesday Book spellings.

Besides sounds that they evidently regarded as ugly or un-pronounceable, the Normans also rejected some English names which contained elements that were distasteful to them. The Essex place called frankly by the Anglo-Saxons *Fulepet*, 'filthy hole' was ennobled by the newcomers into **Beaumont,** 'fair hill', which is hardly an exact translation of the former name, but there may be a touch of irony here. **Belgrave** (Lei) replaced the earlier *Merdegrave*, which the Normans evidently refused to believe meant 'martens' grove'. In Lincolnshire a place known as *Helgelo* ('Helgi's meadow') was renamed **Belleau,** 'fair water'.

The Normans seem to have had an eye for fine scenery, as the names beginning with *Beau-* or *Bel-* testify, but a note of disapproval is occasionally sounded, as in **Malzeard** (WRY), derived from *mal assart*, 'bad clearing'. **Malpas** (Ch), 'difficult passage', is another of this not very numerous group of dis-paraging names. Laudatory names are in the great majority, usually with *Bel-* or *Beau-* in the modern forms. The OF pro-nunciation of this element was closer to 'bew', a sound that survives in many names, e.g. **Beaulieu** (Ha) 'fair place', a variant of which are the Scottish **Beauly** (Inverness-shire) and—with spelling closer to the pronunciation—**Bewdley** (Wo) and **Bewley** (Du). The pronunciation 'bee' is given to the first element in **Beamish** (Du), 'fine mansion', **Beauchief** (Du), 'fine headland'—another instance of which is found in **Beachy Head** (Sx), the second word being obviously unnecessary—and **Belvoir** (Lei), 'fine view'. **Belper** (Db) is 'fair retreat'; **Belasis** (Du—near Billingham), **Bellasis** (Du—near Durham City), **Bellasize** (ERY), and **Belsize** (Hrt, Nth) are the different forms now taken by *Bel assis*, 'beautiful seat'. **Bear Park** (Du) and **Beaurepaire** (Ha) have the same meaning as **Belper; Beaumont** (Cu) has the pronunciation 'bee', but **Beaumont** (E, La) has the sound 'bo' in the first syllable, being, of course 'fine hill'. Impressive, rather than pretty, scenery seems to be alluded to in **Beaufront** (Nb), 'fine brow' and **Beaudesert** (St), 'fine wilderness'. **Beausale** (Nt) and **Beaumanor** (Lei) are self-explanatory. **Belgar** (K) is 'pleasant garden'; **Bewsey** (La) has the same meaning as **Belasis,** but the second element here is OF *sé;* **Butterby** (Du) began its existence as *Beutroue* and so is probably best rendered 'lucky find'.

Not all *Beau-* names have a French origin; **Beausale** (Wa), for instance, is 'Beaw's nook of land', **Beauworth** (Ha) 'bee enclosure', and **Beauxfield** (K) 'Beaw's open land'.

Other wholly French names include **Richmond** (Y), 'rich hill'. This name, like a number of others, was used in imitation of identical names in France, but later itself caused the renaming of a place in Surrey—now **Richmond-upon-Thames**—which until then had been known as **Sheen** ('the shelters'). Monasteries, such as **Grosmont** (NRY, Mon), 'big mountain', were sometimes named after their mother houses in France. **Charterhouse on Mendip** (So) is, of course, from *Chartreuse,* the original *Carthusian* monastery. **Jervaulx** and **Rievaulx,** both in NRY, seem to be translations of the English names 'valley of the river Ure" and 'valley of the river Rye', respectively. **Haltemprice** (ERY), another monastic name, means 'high enterprise'; the same first element (corresponding to Modern French *haut*) occurs in the hybrid name **Haltwhistle** (Nb), 'high river confluence'. **Pontefract** (WRY) was a renaming of *Tateshale;* the alternative form of this name is **Pomfret**, which is closer to the traditional pronunciation of the name. *Pontfreit,* 'broken bridge' was the name bestowed by the Normans, but this was (as was customary) Latinised in legal documents at first to *Fractuspons* and then to *Ponsfractus.* From forms like *Pontefracto,* 'at Pomfret', which would be the most frequently used, the present **Pontefract** resulted, and the situation (until the advent of universal literacy) has been that the written form has been derived from Latin, but the spoken form from French.

In names like **Hamble-le-Rice** (Ha) 'Hamble in the brushwood' the French definite article is a remnant of the phrase *en le,* which survives in **Chapel-en-le-Frith** (Db), 'chapel in the woodland'. Places on Roman roads, curiously, receive this treatment quite often, **-le-Street** being suffixed to mean 'on the Roman road'; examples are **Appleton-le-Street** (NRY), **Chester-le-Street** (Du), and **Wharram-le-Street** (ERY). Other affixes are found in **Bolton le Sands** (La), **Hutton le Hole** (NRY), and **Burgh le Marsh** (L)—all more or less self-explanatory.

But the Norman genius was expressed in a unique way in many of the place-names for which they were responsible.

Perhaps it was a heightened sense of personal identity which led them to use their family names in a special way, not impacted with a suffix, as had sufficed for the Saxons and Danes, or even placed at the end, in the Celtic manner, but standing alone, usually after the existing name, with a kind of aggressive independence. This splendid habit, which has produced so many resounding names, deserves a chapter to itself. That it shall have—the next.

6: FEUDAL AND MANORIAL NAMES

The previous chapters have allowed us to examine the place-names bestowed during about eleven centuries of English history; it might be said that the present chapter will cover all the rest. Probably ninety-eight per cent of existing English place-names originated before 1500, and most of the duplex names now to be examined came into existence between the Norman Conquest and that date.

Names like **Leighton Buzzard** (Bd), **Sydenham Damerel** (D), **Eaton Constantine** (Sa), **Stansted Mountfitchet** (E), and **Ashby de la Zouch** (Le) never fail to impress, but often seem particularly unintelligible. The reason for this is not far to seek. The second word of each of these duplex names is frequently one that occurs in no other place-name, and so the most attentive student of such matters feels baffled. In each of these names this second word is in fact a personal name: the association of the *Busard* family with the Bedfordshire place was first recorded in 1254; **Sydenham Damerel** was held by John D'Albemarle in 1242, and it is interesting to note that the same family name occurs in the early forms of **Hinton Admiral** (Ha); **Eaton Constantine** was tenanted by a family from Contentin in France; **Stansted's** lords originated in Montfiquet in Normandy; Roger de la Zuche was the tenant of **Ashby** in 1200.

Some manorial titles are at least implicit in the Domesday Book record (1086). Although **Tooting Bec** (Sr) was first so called, apparently, in 1255, it was described in 1086 as held by the Abbey of *Bech*, i.e. Bec-Hellouin in Normandy. The other Tooting manor—that of Lower, or South, Tooting was (and is) known as **Tooting Graveney**, being held by Richard de Gravenel in 1215. He is thought to have derived his surname from **Graveney** (K). In Bedfordshire, **Aspley Guise** sets off the rather ordinary name of 'aspen-tree clearing' with the family name of Anselm de Gyse, who held the manor in 1276. **Houghton Conquest**, in the same county, has an even more impressive name. The Conquest family were first recorded as associated with this place, 'farm on a spur of land', in 1223. **Berrick Salome** (O) has an exotic, even Biblical, ring to it. **Berrick** is 'barley farm'; the addition alludes to the family of Almaric de Suleham, 1235, named from **Sulham** (Brk), 'village in narrow valley'. They also held **Britwell Salome**. **Britwell Prior** was held by the Prior of Christchurch, Canterbury, who also held the other Berrick manor, **Berrick Prior**.

The fairly frequent name **Wootton** often receives feudal additions. 'The farm by the wood' is dignified by such great names as Courtney, Bassett, and Rivers. The most venerable name, surely, is **Wootton Wawen** (Wa), traceable to an owner even before the Norman Conquest, one Wagene de Wotton, mentioned in 1050. Other common names similarly distinguished include **Easton**—such as **Easton Bavents** (Sf), **Easton Bassett** (W), **Easton Grey** (W), **Easton Percy** (W), and **Easton Maudit** (Nth). The last name, found also in **Hartley Mauditt** (Ha) is one of the frank nicknames that both Vikings and Normans were fond of; this surname means 'badly educated'. **Herstmonceux** and **Hurstpierpoint** (Sx) differ from most feudal place-names by being single words. The first syllable means 'wooded hill'. The Monceux family, who held their manor from the twelfth century, took their surname from Monceaux, in Calvados, Normandy; the Pierpoints were decidedly senior, however, since Robert de Pierpoint held his *Herst* at the time of Domesday Book. This surname occurs also in **Holme Pierrepont** (Nt). Other examples of names in which the feudal element is impacted with the main name are **Stogumber** and **Stogursey** (So). The main element here is the very common (but rather mysterious) **Stoke**—'place; special (esp. holy) place; dependency'. **Stogumber** has the manorial addition *Gumer* or *Gunner*. **Stogursey** was held in the time of Henry I by William de Curci, a noble from Courcy in Normandy. Many other places called **Stoke** have feudal names added, e.g. **Stoke Edith** (He), named from Queen Edith, widow of Edward the Confessor, who held the manor at the time of the Norman Conquest. **Stoke Abbot** (Do) was held by the Abbot of Sherborne; **Stoke Albany** was held by the family taking its name from the Norman place, Aubigny; **Stoke Damarel** contains a name already mentioned in connection with **Sydenham Dameral** and **Hinton Admiral**. **Stoke Poges** (of Gray's *Elegy* fame) (Bk) was held by Hubert le Pugeis in 1255.

Some manorial additions are in Latin. A name like **Zeal Monachorum** (D) suggests a high degree of virtue among its inhabitants. The addition means 'of the monks', referring to those of Buckfast Abbey. **Zeal** represents OE *sealh*, 'sallow'. **Ashby Puerorum** (L) was assigned for the benefit of the choirboys of Lincoln Cathedral—a purpose alluded to in a 1291 form of the name, *Askeby parvorum chori Lincolniensis*. Many of the

Latin manorial additions relate to ecclesiastical ownership, but it is not entirely convincing to press this as the reason why the name remains in the form used in mediæval documents; many documents were in Latin—at one time, indeed, most were—so that many names were translated in deeds of property. Latin was used in church, it is true, but it was not exclusively the churchmen who had occasion to use the name of their manors. *Esseby Canonicorum* has not survived in that form, but has become **Canons Ashby** (Nth). **Cerne Abbas** and **Milton Abbas** (Do) were monastic manors. **Compton Abbas** (Do) was an ancient possession (from about 871) of Shaftesbury Abbey; the name here means 'abbess's Compton', Shaftesbury being a convent of nuns. Curiously, **Compton Abbas West** is 'abbot's Compton', being the property of Milton Abbey (at **Milton Abbas, Do**). Bishops are alluded to in **Huish Episcopi** and **Kingsbury Episcopi** (So) both manors of the Bishop of Bath and Wells. **Toller Fratrum** (Do) 'Toller of the Brethren', belonged to Forde Abbey.

Other Latin additions, apart from manorial ones, include the fairly common *Magna* and *Parva* ('Great' and 'Little') used to distinguish two places of the same name, e.g. **Ash Magna** and **Parva** (So) and **Appleby Magna** and **Parva** (Lei). Not only are **Wigston Magna** and **Parva** (Lei) a considerable distance apart, they are also of different origins, **Wigston Magna** being formerly *Wichingestone* (1086), 'the Viking's village', and **Wigston Parva**, *Wickgestan* (1002), 'Wicga's stone'. *Ambo* is used when a union takes place of two parishes bearing the same name, e.g., **Wendens Ambo** (E), consisting of **Great** and **Little Wenden**. In **Walton Inferior** and **Superior** (Ch) are the Latin forms replacing the more usual 'lower' and 'upper'. Latin prepositions are used in **Norton juxta Twycross** (Lei), **Langar cum Barnstone** (Nt), **Stratford sub Castle** (W), and **Weston in Gordano** (So), the connectives meaning, respectively, 'near', 'with', 'under', and 'in'. The last-named, together with **Easton in Gordano,** is interesting in that the addition is a whole latinized phrase, **Gordano** being originally OE *gor-denu* 'dirty valley'. Possibly the inhabitants felt such a name needed the 'decent obscurity of a learned language'. Another Somerset **Weston** has a whole Latin phrase affixed—**Weston super Mare**—which tells us that the town is 'on the sea'. **Blandford Forum** (Do) is simply 'Blandford with a market', the affix here being equivalent to the first word in **Chipping Norton** (O); indeed, one early form of the Dorset name was *Cheping Blaneford* (1291).

Again, it has been necessary to make a relatively small selection of all the double place-names of the country. Numerous examples occur in which the manorial element is prefixed, as in **Friern Barnet** (Mx), which belonged to the Hospital of St John

25

of Jerusalem, or **Edith Weston** (R), (cf Stoke Edith, He). Other prefixed expressions also occur, e.g. **Hill Chorlton** (St) and **Brent Pelham** (Hrt), the latter being 'burnt Peotla's village' (*Pelham Combusta* in 1210).

7: NAMES IN WALES AND THE ISLE OF MAN

Though the linguistic threads among the place-names of Wales are not nearly so tangled as those of Scotland, a Welsh map presents a number of interesting features; there are, of course, many Celtic names, but there are not a few English ones also; others are of Scandinavian origin, and some look Welsh but are really English (like **Prestatyn**) or partly English (like **Rhyl**).

The name of the capital, **Cardiff (Caerdydd)**, 'fort on the river' contains the element *caer* that reflects the turbulent history of mediæval Wales. **Caerleon-on-Usk**, 'fort of the legions', retains a memory of Roman occupation. Welsh *llion* represents Latin *legionum*, 'of the legions'—a term that appears in mediæval references to **Chester**. Just as the latter name was modified in its English form, by dropping its first element *Lega*, to avoid confusion with **Leicester,** so **Caerleon** had to be in some way differentiated from the Welsh form of **Chester**—*Caerlleon; ar-Wysg* 'on Usk' was accordingly added. **Caernarvon** means 'fortress in Arfon'—alluding to the tract of country 'facing Anglesey', which is the meaning of the name. **Carmarthen** is also a *caer* name—'fort at Maridunum', *Maridunum* meaning 'sea fort'—but **Cardigan** is not, being simply 'territory of Ceredig'.

Swansea is deceptive. It is not English, though few would think it Welsh. It is, in fact, of Scandinavian origin and means 'Sveinn's island'. **Milford Haven** also has an English look about it, and it, too, is derived from Old Norse. The *-ford*, as in the Irish names **Waterford** and **Wexford,** is for *fjorthr*, 'inlet of the sea'; the whole name is best rendered 'sandy inlet', and it is to be noted that **Haven** was evidently added when the sense of the *-ford* was no longer understood. Similarly *Island* has been added unnecessarily to **Grassholm** and **Skokholm,** respectively 'grass island' and 'island by a deep channel', and to **Caldey,** 'cold island'.

In **Haverfordwest,** although the main part of the name is of Scandinavian origin, an actual ford seems to be alluded to, giving the interpretation 'ford used by goats'—an exact parallel to names in England like Oxford and Hertford. The *west* was an early addition (about 1409), and was to distinguish this name from that of Hereford. **Fishguard** is derived from ON *fiskr*, 'fish' and *garthr*, 'enclosure'; the Scandinavians had a practice of preserving live fish in enclosed areas of water on the seashore, so that they could be taken easily as required. An Isle of Man name, **Fistard**, is of similar origin.

Anglesey, 'Ongull's island', contains a number of places whose names present interesting features. **Holyhead (Caer Gybi)** means 'holy headland'; the Welsh name, 'Cybi's stronghold', actually names the saint who made this such a famous ecclesiastical centre, St Cybi. **Beaumaris** is aptly named, this Norman-French expression meaning 'beautiful marsh'; the town stands on land that was once marshy. On Anglesey also is situated the only place that comes to mind whose very name has been used as a tourist attraction. **Llanfairpwllgwyngyll** is sufficient for normal purposes, such as asking for the telephone exchange, but, intending to break all records, a local enthusiast devised an addition consisting of nearly forty more letters. In full, it is **Llanfairpwllgwyngyllgogerychwyrndrobwllllandysiliogogogoch.** The 'regular' name combines a church dedication with the name of a township: 'St Mary's church in Pwllgwyngyll'. When the anonymous nineteenth-century joker decided to expand the name he ended his monster with the name of the next parish, **Llandysilio**, but in the modified form of the same name applied to a *different* place, in Cardiganshire, where the parish is combined with its neighbour, **Gogo** ('the cave'). **Llandysiliogogo** therefore exists, but not in Anglesey. The middle section, *goger y chwyrn drobwll*, 'near the fierce whirlpool', alludes to Pwll Ceris in the Straits, but is not itself an authentic place-name. The final syllable *-goch* has no significance, and was added just to round off the whole construction—perhaps, desperately, to insist that the name should not be taken seriously. But any record-breaker will take the fancy of the credulous, and it has been said that the hoax has deceived even many Welshmen. **Llanfairpwllgwyngyll** means 'church of (St) Mary near the pool of the white hazel.'

Llan-, meaning 'church', frequently occurs in Welsh names. *Llanfair* ('church of St Mary') names are found so often that distinguishing elements are added. **Llanfairfechan** means 'little church of St Mary'; **Llanfair Caereinion**, 'St Mary's church by the fort of Einion'; **Llanfair-ar-y-Bryn**, 'St Mary's church on the cliff'. Other church dedications are recorded in **Llandudno (St Tudno)**, **Llangollen (St Collen)**, and **Llandeilo (St Teilo)**. **Llandrindod Wells** has a 'church of the Holy Trinity', *Wells* having been added in the nineteenth century when the town was developing as a spa. **Llantrisant** means 'church of three saints'—viz., Dyfodwg, Gwynno, and Illtud. **Llangefni** is 'church near river Cefni'; **Llandovery (Llanymddyfri)** is 'church near the waters'. **Llanbedr Pont Steffan** ('church of St Peter at Stephen's bridge') is perhaps better known in its anglicised form of **Lampeter.**

Another common prefix in Welsh names is *Aber-*, 'river mouth', **Aberystwyth,** 'mouth of river Ystwyth', more exactly describes the site of an early castle, the modern town being on the Rheidol. **Ystwyth** means 'winding river' and occurs also in **Ysbyty Ystwyth,** 'hospice on the Ystwyth'. **Abergele,** 'mouth of the Gele', includes a river name of opposite meaning to Ystwyth. *Gele,* 'spear', alludes to the straightness of the course of the river. **Abergavenny** includes a river name of Romano-British origin, *Gobannion,* '(river) used by smiths'. **Aberaeron,** 'mouth of the Aeron' alludes to the Celtic battle-goddess, whose name was given to this river.

The names of Welsh counties have a variety of origins. Most are Celtic, including some already mentioned as town-names— **Caernarvon, Cardigan, Carmarthen. Pembroke** is 'end land'; **Denbigh** means 'little fort'; **Glamorgan** is 'Morgan's shore'. **Monmouth** (a hybrid name as befits a border county) takes its name from the town at the 'mouth of the Mynwy'. **Brecknock (Brecon)** is 'territory of Brychan'; **Merioneth,** 'territory of Meirion'. **Montgomery** is a feudal name, taken from the baron's home of Montgommery in Calvados. **Flint** and **Radnor** are of English origin; the former is simply the geological term, though broadly applied to any hard rock; the latter is 'red hillside'.

Town names of English origin include **Newtown, Middletown,** and **Newport,** which are self-explanatory. **Hawarden** is 'high enclosure'; **Rhyl** is English 'hill', with the Welsh definite article *yr* prefixed, and so the name must be rendered simply 'the hill'—paradoxically, since the elevation is but slight. **Prestatyn,** from OE *prēosta-tūn,* 'priests' village', has arrived at its present form because of the Welsh habit of stressing the last syllable but one; in England, names of this origin have developed into **Preston. Presteigne** means 'household or community of priests'. **Chepstow** is 'market place'; **Mounton** means 'village belonging to the monks', viz. those of Chepstow Priory.

Tintern is a Celtic name, meaning 'king's fort'. The same element is found in **Tenby,** which looks Scandinavian but is, in fact, wholly Welsh, meaning 'little fort'.

The element *pont*, 'bridge', appears in a number of Welsh names. **Pont-y-Pridd** means 'bridge of the earthen house', **Pontypool,** 'bridge of the pool'—the last element being the English word *pool*. **Pontnewydd** is 'new bridge'; **Pontfaen** is 'stone bridge'. Two places are called **Talybont,** meaning 'end of the bridge', corresponding to the Glamorgan name **Bridgend. Pontarddulais** means 'bridge over the river Dulais'; this river name is of similar origin to a number called **Douglas,** meaning 'black stream'.

Pwllheli is 'salt pool'; **Harlech,** 'fine stone'; **Bangor,** 'crossbar in hurdle'. **Bala** means 'outlet from the lake'; **Dolgellau** means 'meadow of the cells'. **Ffestiniog** is 'defence territory', and **Blaenau Ffestiniog** 'heights of Ffestiniog'. **Towyn** points to its location, and means 'sea shore'. **Betws-y-Coed** means 'prayer house in the wood'; **Rhuddlan** is 'red bank', and **Rhuthun,** 'red fort'. **Merthyr Tydfil** is 'grave of St Tudful'.

Local government reorganisation has brought about the revival of some ancient names, though they are applied to areas different in extent from those to which they formerly belonged. **Powys** means 'territory of the dwellers in the open country'. **Gwynedd** means 'region of the hunters'. **Clwyd** is 'hurdle place'; **Gwent** means 'market'. **Dyfed** is the tribal name, *Demetae*.

The Isle of Man has less in common with Wales, perhaps, than with Ireland or Scotland, since Manx belongs to the Goidelic group of Celtic languages, whereas Welsh is Brythonic. There are also many names of Norse origin. **Peel,** 'fortress', is named from the castle. This name began its life with a less dignified meaning, since originally it was merely 'palisade', but it was extended eventually to refer to every kind of fortification. **Bride** and **Andreas** are dedication names, in full **Kirkbride** and **Kirkandreas,** 'church of St Bridget' and 'church of St Andrew'. **Ramsey** (ON *Ramsá*) is named from a stream now called the Lickney stream. The Old Norse name means 'wild garlic stream'. **Maughold Head** is a promontory named after St Machud, the tutelary saint of the parish of **Kirk Maughold. Laxey** is ON *Laxá*, 'salmon river'.

Baldrine is from Manx *Balley drine*, 'farm of the blackthorn'. **Douglas**, already mentioned in connection with similar Welsh names, means 'black stream'. **Ballakillingan** is 'farm of (St) Fingan's church'; **Ballabeg** is 'little farm'; **Ballameanagh** is 'middle farm'. **Jurby** is probably 'Dyri's homestead'. **Sulby** is 'Soli's farm'. **Stroin Vuigh** is 'yellow headland'.

The innumerable minor names of the island have been studied in greater detail, probably, than those of any other area of comparable size, and for a full discussion of them an interested reader may turn to J. J. Kneen's *Place-Names of the Isle of Man*, and to the articles by Dr. M. Gelling in the *Journal of the Manx Museum* in 1970 and 1971.

8: IRISH AND SCOTTISH PLACE-NAMES

In the modern Irish language, the name for the westernmost of the British Isles is **Éire**; the early name was *Eriu* (whose dative case, *Erinn*, has also been regularly used in the past) meaning 'western place'. The English name **Ireland** is deceptively similar in form to **England**, but whereas the latter is from *Engla-land*,

'land of the Angles', the former is an attempt to give an English dress to the Gaelic name, so that it can only be rendered by 'land of Éire'.

Politically, the island is now divided between the Republic of Ireland in the south, and Northern Ireland, which is a part of the United Kingdom. Northern Ireland is often called **Ulster**, though it in fact comprises only six of the eight counties of the ancient province. **Ulster**, like two more of the provinces, has a name of mixed descent, Scandinavian *stathr*, 'place', being added to the Irish tribal name, *Ulaidh*. One of the six counties is **Down**, 'fortress'; also derived from Irish *dun* are **Downpatrick**, 'St Patrick's fortress', and **Dundrum**, 'fort on the long hill'. **Armagh**, the name of both a county and a city, is 'Macha's height', commemorating one of three women named in Irish legendary history, though it is not certain which one. North of County Down is **Antrim** ('one holding'), containing within its boundaries the capital of the province, **Belfast**, 'ford at the sandbank'. Two places in Antrim, **Ballymena** and **Ballycastle**, include the frequent Irish element, *baile*, 'town', being 'middle town' and 'town by the castle' respectively. **Ballymoney**, in this and other counties, is 'town with a shrubbery'. But **Ballyclare** has a different origin and is 'pass of the plain'; more than one town and a county have the name **Clare**, 'plain'. **Carrickfergus**, 'rock of Fergus', shows the characteristic order of elements, unlike the normal mode for English names of placing the personal name first, and resembling names in England like **Aspatria**. **Larne** is from a personal name, Lathair (a legendary character). County **Derry** is named from the town, meaning 'oak wood', the extended form **Londonderry** commemorating the association of London merchants with the town from the time of James I. **Coleraine** is 'nook of the ferns'. The name of County **Tyrone** perpetuates the memory of Owen, the ancestor of the O'Neills; the lands of this hero, who died in A.D. 465, were much more extensive than the present-day county, the name of which signifies 'Owen's territory'. **Clogher**, a name found in this county and in Mayo, means 'stony place'.

Fermanagh recalls 'the men of Monach'; this tribe, descended from Monach, were Leinstermen who had to leave that province after killing its king, Enna. Another personal name, that of Cethlenn, wife of the great chief Balor, is found in **Enniskillen**, 'island of Cethlenn.'

Donegal, in the Irish Republic, is 'fortress of the foreigners'. According to the Annals of Ulster, a Danish fortress was destroyed here in 1159. Elsewhere in Ireland, *Gall*, 'foreigner', usually relates to Englishmen, but **Galway** means 'stony place'.

Monaghan is in Irish *Muineachan*, 'little shrubbery', being the diminutive form of *muine*, found in **Ballymoney** (above) and in **Moniven** in Co. Galway, which is 'shrubbery of the mead', doubtless alluding to the brewing there of that drink.

Sligeach, the Irish name for **Sligo**, was originally the name of the river; it means 'abounding in shells'. **Collooney**, in the same county, is 'nook of the thicket'; **Tobercurry** contains an element frequently occurring, *tobar*, 'well'. The Co. Sligo name actually means 'well of the caldron'. In Co. **Mayo** ('plain of the yews') are found **Ardnaree** and **Ballina**. The two places are very close, the second meaning 'ford mouth'; the former means 'height of the executions', as it was the place where were hanged the Four Maels, murderers of Guaire Aidhne, king of Connaught.

In the far west of Ireland is the district of **Connemara**, which takes its name from the descendants of Conmac, son of Fergus, ex-king of Ulster, and Maev, queen of Connaught. The *Conmacne*, as this tribe were called, held several territories; the one by the sea was called *Conmaicne-mara*, 'seaside *Conmaicne*',

Clare means 'level place'. Within the boundaries of this county is much of the great **Lough Derg**, 'lake of the red'—dyed according to legend, with the blood of Eochy MacLuchta, king of south Connaught, who plucked out his own eye at the request of the poet Aithirne. The river **Shannon** is named from an ancient goddess. **Limerick** is a 'barren spot'; **Roscommon** is 'Coman's wood', from the saint who founded a monastery there and died in the seventh century. **Tipperary** is 'well of Ara', alluding to the ancient territory in which the town is situated. **Leitrim** is 'grey ridge'. **Longford,** despite its Saxon appearance, is a completely Irish name, meaning 'fortified house'. In Co. Westmeath is to be found **Mullingar**, 'crooked mill'. In the far west of that county, on the river Shannon, **Athlone** is to be found—the 'ford of Luan'. Among the towns of Co. Offaly are **Tullamore**, 'big hill' and **Banagher**, 'peaked hill'. Co. **Leix** is named after a certain Ulster chieftain, Lughaidh Laeighseach, who came to the aid of the king of Leinster in the second century A.D. In return the king granted him extensive lands in this area, now called by the tribal name *Laois*. **Abbeyleix** is accordingly self-explanatory, and another famous ecclesiastical centre is nearby—**Durrow**, 'oak plain'. **Kilkenny**, 'cell of Cainnech', commemorates the saint known in Scotland as Kenneth. **Freshford** is an instance of a translated name—and a bad translation, moreover, the Irish name being *Achadhur*, 'fresh field'. **Waterford** and **Wexford,** both giving their names to the respective counties, are of Scandinavian origin. The former is 'inlet of the wether' and the latter 'sea-washed inlet'. **Lismore** (Co. Waterford) is 'big fort'; **Tramore**, on the coast, 'big strand'. **Tralee,** in Co. Kerry. is 'shore of the river Lee'. **Killarney,** in the same county, is 'church of the sloes'. **Listowel** is one of a group of fort-names, being 'fort of Tuathal'; others are **Liscarroll** (Co. Cork) and **Liscahane** (Co. Kerry)—'fort of Carroll' and 'fort of Cathan' respectively. The eldest son of Fergus and Maev was Ciar, and it was he who gave his name to **Kerry. Cork,** the adjoining county, bears the name of the city founded near St Finbar's monastery in *Corcach-mor-mumhan*, 'the great marsh of Munster'. At the extreme west and east edges of this county are two bays: **Bantry** and **Youghal.** The former perpetuates the memory of the *Beanntraighe*, 'race of Beann', descendants of one of the sons of Conor MacNessa, king of Ulster. The latter is 'yew-wood', from an ancient wood on the hill on which the town was built. **Cloyne** was *Cluain-uamha*, 'the meadow of the cave'. **Mallow** is 'plain of the rock'; **Cobh** is 'the cove', the English word attractively disguised in Irish spelling. **Skibbereen** is 'place frequented by boats', and so may the name **Kinsale** imply, since it is 'head of the brine'. The town of **Carlow** is said to be so called because the river formed there a 'fourfold lake'. **Wicklow** is another Scandinavian name, meaning 'Viking's meadow', the same termination (ON *ló*) being found in **Arklow,** 'Arnkell's meadow'. **Kildare** is 'church of the oak tree', the oak alluded to having been, according to an ancient account, much loved by St Brigid.

Leixlip, from Old Norse *Laxhlaup*, 'salmon leap', is named from a cataract on the river Liffey. **Naas,** said to have been the earliest residence of the kings of Leinster, means 'assembly place'; **Maynooth** means 'plain of Nuadhat'.

The capital of the Republic, **Dublin,** bears a name originally bestowed on the part of the river Liffey on which it was built, meaning 'black pool'. In Irish it is now called *Baile Atha Cliath*, 'town at the hurdle ford'. **Lucan** is 'place of elms'. **Dun Laoghaire** commemorates Laoghaire, who was king of Ireland from 428 to 458. **Trim,** in Co. Meath, is 'elder-tree place', from the trees that grew near an ancient ford across the river Boyne. **Trummery,** in Co. Antrim, has the same meaning. **Kells** is the much eroded form of *Ceanannus*, 'chief residence'; **Drogheda** is 'bridge by a ford'.

Scotia, in the earliest records, was the name applied to Ireland, for the very good reason that the Scots lived there. In course of time, however, both the people and the name were transferred to the northern part of Britain. The ancient name, **Caledonia,** after much discussion among Celtic scholars, is now usually explained as '(land of the) battle-cry'. The name is incorporated in **Dunkeld,** 'fort of the Caledonians', and in the mountain name, **Schiehallion,** in Gaelic *Sidh Chailleann*, 'fairy hill of the Caledonians'.

Ireland was able to put up a greater resistance to foreign influence on her place-names than Scotland, where there are innumerable examples of Scandinavian and English words constituting, or incorporated in, the names. The **Shetland Islands,** for example, bear a Norse name, 'hilt land'; the name of the **Orkneys** is hybrid, for to the ancient *Orc* has been added Scandinavian *ey*, 'island', the *n* probably surviving from the Gaelic *inis*, 'island'. This name is usually interpreted 'boar islands', probably alluding to the boar as a kind of totem. The most northerly county of Scotland, **Caithness,** also bears an animal name, 'cape of the Cat (tribe)'—originally North Cape, but now applied to the whole territory as far as **Sutherland,** which the tribe also occupied. Not merely the termination, but the whole name here, is of Norse origin, and this was the 'south land' to those who were based in Orkney. Meaning either 'promontory' or 'moor', the Gaelic-named **Ross** is divided into **Easter Ross** and **Wester Ross,** 'eastern' and 'western Ross', these additions being Scandinavian. **Cape Wrath** may appear to be appropriate, but it is in fact *Hvarf*, 'turning of the land'. *Tarvodunon*, the early Celtic name for Dunnet Head, means 'bull fort', a name that sheds some light on the meaning of **Thurso.** The Scandinavian termination and general appearance of this name belie its nature; it seems to have begun life as a translation of *Tarvodubron*, 'bull's water'—*Thjorsá*, but was adapted to *Thorsá* because of the frequency with which references to Thor occur in place-names. **Dounreay** is 'fort on a mound'. **Durness** is 'deer promontory'. **Wick** is from Norse *vik*, 'bay'. **Helmsdale, Brora,** and **Golspie** are all of Scandinavian origin, and mean respectively 'Hjalmund's valley', 'bridge river', and 'Gulli's village'. **Lairg,** however, is Gaelic: 'thigh'. **Gairloch** is 'short loch', and **Dornoch,** also Gaelic, is 'pebbly place', with the implication that the pebbles were of a size to fill the fist (*dorn*), and therefore of some utility as weapons. **Nairn** is named from its river, the appellation being a pre-Celtic one and meaning 'flowing water'. **Dingwall** reminds us of the Scandinavian custom of government by means of local assemblies; this town is on the site of the field where one of these was held, and the name, like **Thingwall** (Ch), **Thingwall** (La), **Tynwald** (Isle of Man), and indeed **Thingvellir** (Iceland) must be rendered 'field of assembly'.

It has now been demonstrated (by Dr A. B. Taylor) that the name **St Kilda**—in the outermost Hebrides—does not, in fact, commemorate a saint at all. Much effort has been spent in trying to identify this elusive holy person, to little purpose, for reasons that now become apparent. Just as in England the name **Sarum** arose from a misreading of the abbreviated form of *Sarisberi* **(Salisbury),** so this new saint was added to the calendar from a mistaken reading of *Skildar* ('shields') on early maritime charts. The appropriateness of the name is confirmed by the appearance on the horizon of the gentle arcs of St Kilda's uplands, convincingly resembling Norse shields laid flat on the earth.

Inverness, 'mouth of the Ness', is one of the numerous group of names beginning with Inver- (Gaelic *Inbhir-*), 'river mouth'. **Lossiemouth,** however, adds English -mouth to its Gaelic river-name, which means 'river of herbs'. **Banff** presents difficulties in interpretation, but 'pig' seems to be the meaning now agreed on. One difficulty is that, although animal names are used of rivers in Wales, this is not usual in Scotland. The Gaelic name, *Banbh*, is associated with *Banba*, a Gaelic poetic name—one might almost say pet-name—for Ireland, and 'little Ireland' is the usual interpretation of **Elgin** in the adjoining county of **Moray** ('sea settlement').

Keith is Celtic in origin, but Brittonic and not Goidelic. The Scots from Ireland brought with them their Goidelic language, but the earlier inhabitants used dialects akin to those of the Britons of the South—and, of course, to modern Welsh. The name means 'wood' and may be compared with names like **Chetwode** in England. **Dalkeith** in Midlothian, 'meadow of the wood' has a Gaelic word prefixed. **Peterhead,** 'St Peter's head-land' is an example of an English name, rare in this part of Scotland. **Aberdeen** and **Arbroath** both include the Brittonic element *Aber-* 'river mouth', being respectively 'mouth of river Don' and 'mouth of Brothock'. **Montrose** is 'moorland on the promontory'; **Kirriemuir** has reference to land measurement, the first element being *Ceathramh*, 'fourth part', i.e., a quarter of a davoch—itself equivalent to 192 Scottish acres of arable, together with a sufficiency of rough grazing. **Aberfeldy** and **Pitlochry** have in common a non-Goidelic origin, but each has a separate interest. Unlike most *Aber-* names, **Aberfeldy** does not include the name of the river concerned (which is, in fact, **Moness** Burn—*i mbun eas*, 'near waterfalls') but alludes to Peallaidh, a water demon. The town name is best rendered 'demon-haunted river mouth'. An impressive list of a hundred or more names commencing with *Pit-*, from Pitalmit to Pityoulish, presents us with an array of the names that have caused one of the liveliest of long arguments among scholars. The dispute includes a number of other more general ones, such as the identity of the Pictish people, whether they were one people or more, what language or languages they spoke, their relations with their neighbours, and so on, and we might say that the whole debate is crystallised in these interesting names. For a non-specialist it is sufficient to know that all are agreed that the first element means 'portion', and that **Pitlochry** is interpreted 'stony ground portion', with a possible reference to stepping stones. Other examples of this type of name are **Pitmaduthy** (Ross-shire), 'Macduff's portion', **Pettymuck** (Aberdeenshire), 'pig portion', **Pettyvaich**, 'share with cow-shed', **Pitcowden**, 'hazel portion', and **Pittenweem** (Fife), 'share of the cave'.

Perth, 'thicket', is a further example of the group of Brythonic words found in Scottish place-names; **Brechin** also belongs to these, with the further interest that it consists merely of a personal name—Brychan—implying possession by the man named. **Peebles**, a third member of the group, means 'temporary dwellings'. **Glasgow**, also British in origin, means 'green hollow'; the second element is found in *Lithgow*, 'damp hollow', referred to in **Linlithgow**, 'lake of Lithgow'. **Dumbarton**, 'fortress of the Britons', was the chief settlement of the Strathclyde Britons, whose own name for their capital was *Alclut*, 'rock of Clyde'. The county-name is spelt **Dunbartonshire**.

Fort William, Fort Augustus, and **Fort George** commemorate, if anything, English military activity in Scotland during the eighteenth century. The oldest of these garrisons was founded in 1690 and named in honour of King William III; the second received the name of Prince William Augustus, Duke of Cumberland, and the third that of King George II. All things considered the survival of these names is perhaps an object of wonder.

Oban is, appropriately enough, 'little bay'. **Argyll** is 'coastland of the Gael'. **Bute** appears to be '(island of) fire', referring to signal fires. **Mull** is 'lofty island', and **Tobermory**, 'well of St Mary'. **Ayr**, *Inbhir-àir*, has retained an important prefix in Gaelic but lost it in English. Since *Inbhir-* (=Inver-) means 'mouth of a river', the interpretation 'river' for the second element makes for a rather repetitive rendering of the whole name, until it is realised that *àir* would have been no more than a name to the Gaels who added the prefix, and its significance would have already been lost. *Ayr* is, in fact, one of the primitive, pre-Celtic river names to be found throughout Britain. **Stirling** is a name for which no interpretation is offered, though it may be noted that it is thought that a river name forms the first element.

About the second element of **Edinburgh** there is no dispute: it is undoubtedly OE *burh*, 'fortification, fortified place', but there is serious disagreement about the first component. One view is that it represents the original (Celtic) name of the place, to which the explanatory -*burh* was added by Angles, the Celtic *Dun* being prefixed to *Eidyn* by Britons and Gaels. But partisans of a different view insist that the evidence of forms like *Eduenesburg* and *Edwinesburg* supports the idea that this was a fortress established or defended by King Edwin. Further argument adduces historical evidence to rebut this theory, but the upshot is that if **Edinburgh** does not mean 'fortress of (King) Edwin' nobody knows what it does mean, since no interpretation of *Eidyn*, as an original Celtic name, has been offered.

Airdrie and **Hamilton** are difficult names, and no interpretation is here put forward; **Motherwell** is thought to be 'Our Lady's well', but there is considerable doubt about the meaning. **Lanark** is a British name, meaning 'glade'. **Duns** and **Largs** are probably names of Gaelic origin to which English *-s* for the plural has been added; they mean 'hill-forts' and 'slopes' respectively. **Lothian**, the name of the ancient province, is thought to be derived from the name of its founder Leudonus; the three counties into which it is now divided are East Lothian or **Haddington** ('estate of Hada's kin'), Edinburgh or Mid-Lothian, and Linlithgow or West Lothian. **Bo'ness** is a name that arouses curiosity; in full (though it is never so pronounced) it is Borrowstounness—'point of Borrowstoun', the latter name being 'Beornweard's village'.

9: FORESTS, HILLS AND RIVERS

Whatever else Roman Britain may have lacked, it suffered no shortage of timber. Thick forests covered much of the countryside, and the few settlements within their bounds were to be found in natural or man-made clearings. The survival of so few forest-names down to the present day amply demonstrates the size of the destruction that has taken place. Very few names spring readily to mind: **Sherwood Forest** (Nt) is probably the best-known; the earliest record of the name is dated 986, when it took the form *Scyryuda*, probably for *Scyrwuda*, since it was *Scirwuda* in documents dated a little later, meaning 'wood belonging to the shire', possibly because at least some of the population of the county early had the right of pasturing their swine in the forest.

In the north-west Midlands, **The Lyme** is now a rather vague region taking in parts of Staffordshire, Shropshire, Cheshire and south-east Lancashire; there is early evidence that this was once a great forest, and the name is usually explained as 'the elmy place'. **Ashton Under Lyne** (La) and **Newcastle Under Lyme** (St) are named with reference to the area. Also in the Midlands was the forest from which **Lichfield** (St) took its name; this has been briefly discussed in Chapter 3. The extant forest-names in Northamptonshire, however, are all of later origin than these. **Rockingham Forest** takes its name from the town, 'homestead of

Hroc's people'. **Cliffe Forest** is likewise named after a town, this time **King's Cliffe**, 'hill slope'. **Salcey Forest** is 'place of willows', the name being from OFr *salceie* and first recorded in 1206. **Whittlewood Forest** takes its name from one Witela.

Wyre Forest was once a great area taking in much of western Worcestershire. The tribe of the Wigoran, who gave their name to **Worcester**, are commemorated in this name. **Selwood Forest** (So) is 'sallow wood'. **The New Forest** (Ha) has been so called for nearly nine hundred years, having been reserved as a hunting ground for William I. **Galtres Forest** (NRY) is 'boar wood'; **Ashdown Forest** (Sx) is 'ash-tree hill'. **The Weald** (K, Ha) occurs in OE as *Andredesweald*, 'forest of Andred', incorporating the name of a British town, Anderida, whose meaning is uncertain.

Some important river-names have been discussed in earlier chapters, but a few more may be mentioned here. The **Tyne** (Cu, Nb, Du), like the numerous rivers **Avon,** is simply 'river'. The **Severn** was on record early, being mentioned in the *Annals* of Tacitus. The British form of the name was *Sabrina*, which developed through *Saverna* to the modern name, which possibly means 'milky'. There are several rivers to which the name **Humber** is applied, in addition to the great estuary (of the rivers **Ouse** and **Trent**) which acts as an important county and regional boundary. The meaning of the name is obscure, but it has been suggested that it is a complimentary name, 'good river', intended to placate a natural force that, without such flattery, might overwhelm those living near it. There are also several rivers **Dove**. This name, 'dark one', suggests that either the water is clouded or stained, or that the course of the river is through a deep valley. The river **Cam** has taken its modern name from **Cambridge**, which, as has been seen, is a development of the earlier *Grantebrige*, 'bridge over the Granta'. The river name means 'shallow one' or, possibly, 'muddy river'. **Chelmer** is another example, like **Cam**, of 'back formation', i.e., the bestowing of part of the name of a town upon a river. The town in this case is **Chelmsford** (E), which means 'Ceolmær's ford', Ceolmær, of course, being a personal name. The 'back formation' process, however, interprets the name as 'Chelmer ford', and thus attributes the first name to the river. Another instance of this is **Chelt** (Gl), from **Cheltenham**. **Wandle** (Sr) is similarly named from **Wandsworth.**

Instead of prefixing the word 'river' as we do today, the Anglo-Saxons would often add a name like *burna* or *brōc* at the end, both of these words meaning 'brook'. OE *ea*, 'river', which has become **Eye** and **Yeo**, terminates **Waveney**, 'fen river', and **Mersey**, 'boundary river', the latter having formerly divided the Anglo-Saxon kingdom of Northumbria from that of Mercia. The importance of streams as boundaries is also indicated by such names as **Marlbrook** (Sa) and **Meersbrook** (Db, WRY). **Tyburn** (Mx) has a similar meaning, though the first element is a different one; this stream was in 959 the boundary of Westminster Abbey's Middlesex territory. The name was changed to **Marybourn,** into which *le* unwarrantably intruded, to make the place-name **Marylebone. Tachbrook** (Wa, Wo) is the name of two streams, and is also interpreted 'boundary stream', the first element meaning 'marker, indicator'. Personal names are found in some river names, e.g., **Cottesbrooke** and **Lilbourne** (Nth). In other names, the first element denotes some quality of the water, e.g. **Saltburn** (NRY) and **Colburn** (NRY)—the latter being 'cool stream'. Clear water is indicated in **Sherburn** (ERY), **Shirburn** (O), and **Shirebrook** (Db), whereas that of **Fulbrook** (Bk, Wa) and **Skidbrook** (L) was decidedly the opposite. Birds are alluded to in **Cranborne** (Do) and **Gusborne** (K)—referring to herons and the goose respectively.

Other suffixes in river names include -*water* and -*lake*. The **Whitewater** (Ha, Brk) is, believe it or not, a tributary of the **Blackwater. Loudwater** (Bk) is appropriately named; it does indeed produce an incessant noise. **Shiplake** (O) is 'sheep stream'; **Fenlake** (Bd) is 'stream flowing through a fen'.

Hill-names of Celtic origin include **Malvern** (Wo), 'bare hill' and **Bredon** (Wo). The latter is derived from British *briga*, 'hill', with the English suffix, also meaning 'hill', added. Another 'duplicated' name is **Brill** (Co), in which the second element is OE *hyll*, instead of *dun* as in **Bredon**. British *penno*, 'summit' is found in some hill-names. **Pendle Hill** (La) is interesting as a 'triplicated' form: to the British word, which would have been sufficient to denote a hill, was added OE *hyll*, producing the form **Pendle**. In course of time neither the Celtic nor the Old English element was felt to have more than a naming function, and users felt it necessary to clarify the nature of **Pendle** by adding modern **Hill**. It is worth noting that **Pennine,** despite its apparent relationship with names embodying the element *penno*, seems to have been introduced, if not actually invented, only in the eighteenth century. Another British word for 'mountain' is found in names like **Mynde** (He) and **Longmynd** (Sa), the latter being a long ridge. This element also occurs in **Mendip,** the second element of which is obscure, but may be OE *hop*, 'valley'. The **Chiltern** Hills also bear a name of British origin, but, apart from noting that the name was originally applied to a forest somewhat greater in extent than the range of hills, it is necessary to say that little is certain about the origin or meaning of the name; one suggestion is that the first syllable represents a

British word meaning 'high'. The **Cotswolds,** however, had an English origin, the second element being OE (Anglian) *wald*, 'upland forest'. A personal name, *Cod,* constitutes the first element. The **Wolds** of the East Midlands have a name of the same origin.

Among the Norse words occurring in mountain names is *fell,* used a great deal in the Lake District. In **Sca Fell** (Cu) the original Celtic hill-name, meaning 'bald hill', is reinforced with the Scandinavian element. Tree-names are found with this element, e.g., **Ash Fell** and **Bire Fell** (We). **Whinfell** (Cu) is 'hill overgrown with furze'. Old Norse *skuti* 'overhanging rock' occurs in **Scout Crag** (We) and in **Kinder Scout** (Db), the first word of which is probably of Celtic origin and means 'high hill.'

10: FIELD-NAMES, STREET-NAMES, AND SCOPE FOR PRACTICAL WORK

In addition to the names of natural features and of cities, towns, and villages, there are countless other names of places accessible within a restricted area. Only on a large-scale plan, or listed in a town guide, are street names to be found; only on certain maps and estate documents are fields ever labelled with their names. Both types of name have great interest and both can be profitably studied, but so vast are the numbers concerned that the small sample for which there is room here must represent a tiny fraction of the total.

That fields should have names at all sometimes comes as a surprise to the town-dweller. Inspection of the parish tithe map, or the perusal of the particulars of sale of farm land, however, will reveal the existence of land bearing such names as **Eleven Acres, Bull Piece, Priestholme, Oakshot Meadow, Browne's Close,** and **Upper Carr Field.** This random selection offers a fair sample of some of the classes of name commonly met with.

Acreage names are very common—to the extent, occasionally, of constituting about half the names in a parish. In the form **Eleven Acres** or **Eleven Acre Close,** the measurement is usually quite accurate; names such as **Eleven Acre Meadow or Eleven Acre Wood,** however, will be found usually to bear no relation to actual extent. The reason for this is that arable land is the criterion; adjacent meadows or woods are often given the same name as the ploughed land, and if this happens to be called by an acreage name, that name is applied to the pasture or wood irrespective of its own area.

Cattle and sheep are frequently alluded to in names of fields, quite often with reference to the actual way the land was used. The bull would be kept apart from the herd—usually on quite a small piece of land—hence names like **Bull Piece** or **Bull Pingle.** Other names of this type include **Calves' Close, Cow Pasture, Sheep Close,** and **Lambcotes.**

Names of owners or occupiers may be included in field-names. Glebe land will have names such as **Parson's Piece, Priest Meadow, Vicarage Close,** or **Priestholme.** Surnames of owners or tenants at the time of the enclosure of the common fields occur in such names as **Jacob's Piece, Fremantle Close,** and **Browne's Close.**

Oakshot Meadow, although applied to enclosed land, refers back to the days of strip cultivation in the open fields. The great fields under that system were divided into groups of strips or holdings; these divisions of the common field were called furlongs or shots and were given individual names, such as **Rye Furlong, Stoneshot, Wheathill,** or **Oakshot.** These names, like those applied to modern enclosed land, often related to the actual use of the land, but some names, especially those of major crops, which would of course be sown in rotation on all the arable land, appear to have been bestowed arbitrarily.

The process of enclosure consisted in the allocation of large pieces of land in single holdings in place of a number of separate strips distributed through all the great fields of a parish. Such a consolidation might mean that an individual tenant would receive a whole furlong as his allocation; this might retain its original name, e.g. **Stone Furlong,** or be renamed **Stone Furlong Close.** Another way an original name might be adapted was as **First Stone Furlong, Second Stone Furlong,** and **Third Stone Furlong;** this indicated that the particular furlong was divided among three owners. Sometimes the great fields themselves were divided along different boundaries from those that had previously parted the constituent furlongs. This arrangement gave rise to such names as **Upper Carr Field, Middle Carr Field,** and **Lower Carr Field,** when the original name had been **Carr Field.**

Street-names are within the experience of everyone. Again, numbers are too great to allow a summary treatment. Suffice it to say that it is not outside the scope of any interested individual to collect and study the street-names of his own town, and to trace the origin of many, if not all, of them. **King Street,** for example, may commemorate a king associated with the town, or, more often, honour some former citizen bearing that surname. Historical events may indicate when certain streets were built (or renamed), and names like **Waterloo Terrace, Alma Road,** and **Jubilee Street** suggest the kind of questions to be asked. Names relating to buildings, e.g. the common **Church Street, Castle Street, Bridge Road,** and **Station Road,** may allude to buildings no longer in existence, and features of local history can therefore be uncovered by an investigation that begins with street-names. Other streets may be named after the fields over which they were built—names like **Long Acre** are reminders of this.

The same techniques are employed in the interpretation of field-names and street-names as are used in general place-name study. It is necessary to collect early forms of existing names and to study these alongside the topographical and social conditions of the place as well as in accordance with the laws of language development, to arrive at any definite or probable interpretation. Provided the greatest care is exercised in the recording of all the relevant information, e.g. the actual spelling of names in a document, as well as the date, description, and location of the document itself, any enthusiast can make a real contribution to this body of knowledge. Dated extracts from directories, lists of field-names from old maps, or other catalogues of information, can prove of the greatest utility; if the individual does not feel equal to attempting an explanation of the names he collects, he will often find a body of collaborators with the requisite knowledge among them. Co-operative projects like this are in progress in many parts of the country; taking part in one of them, or even undertaking a piece of solitary research, will rapidly produce the rewards obtainable from discovering place-names.

11: GLOSSARY OF TECHNICAL TERMS

ADDITION
A separate word acting as a distinguishing mark in certain place-names. The addition may precede or follow the place-name proper, and frequently serves to particularise places bearing common names, e.g. **Stoke, Sutton, Newton, Norton, Buckland,** and **Stratford.** Additions may be descriptive, as in **Stony Stratford** (Bk) or **Stoke Dry** (Ru); referential, as in **Severn Stoke** (Wo) or **Sutton by Middlewich** (Ch); feudal or manorial, as in **Newton Harcourt** (Lei) or **Bishop's Sutton** (Ha); dedicatory, as in **St Michael Caerhays** (Co) ('St Michael's barley town') or **Chalfont St Giles** (Bk) ('Cheadel's spring, with church dedicated to St Giles'); or a district name, as in **Hemel Hempstead** (Hrt) ('homestead in *Hamel*, i.e. broken country') or **Sutton in Ashfield** (Nt) (i.e. 'in the open land with ash trees').

AFFIX
Alternative term for ADDITION (q.v.).

BACK-FORMATION

The use of part of a town-name as that of a river, irrespective of the original meaning of the part so used. In **Wandsworth** (GL) and **Chelmsford** (E) the first elements are the personal names Wendel and Ceolmær, but the river names **Wandle** and **Chelmer** have been devised, as though the town names belonged to the large group of names formed from river names followed by appropriate endings—e.g. **Exminster** or **Yarmouth**. The naming process is thus a reversal of the more usual one.

COMPOUND

Either a place-name consisting of two ELEMENTS (e.g. **Bristol**, 'bridge place', made up of OE *brycg* and *stōw*), *or* (paradoxically) an ELEMENT consisting of two THEMES (e.g. OE *hām-stede*, 'homestead, site of a dwelling', comprising the two themes, *hām* and *stede*, but regarded as a unitary element in names like **Finchampstead**, Brk—'homestead frequented by finches').

ELEMENT

One of the units composing a place-name. An element may be a common noun, e.g. OE *swīn*, 'pig', *slīm*, 'mud', or *stān*, 'stone', all of which may combine with OE *ford*, 'ford', as in **Swinford** (Bk, K), **Slimeford** (Co), **Stanford** (Brk, E); or it may be an adjective, e.g., OE *brād*, 'broad', *rūh*, 'rough', or *walt*, 'unsteady', which produce **Bradford** (WRY), **Rufford** (La), and **Walford** (Do). Personal names may also be elements as in **Aylesbury** (Bk), 'Ægel's fortified place', or **Bloxham** (O), 'Blocc's village'.

FOLK-NAME

A place-name consisting simply of the name of the tribe, e.g. **Norfolk**, **Devon**, or **Barking** (GL)—the latter meaning 'Berica's people'.

HABITATION-NAME

A place-name explicitly designating a dwelling-place, as distinct from a natural feature, e.g. in **Brafferton** (Du), 'enclosure at the broad ford', the element *tūn* alludes to a habitation, whereas **Bradford,** strictly, refers to a geographical feature, a 'broad ford'.

HYBRID

A place-name consisting of elements from two languages—often Old English and Old Norse, e.g. **East Garston** (Brk), 'Esgar's village', in which a Scandinavian personal name is followed by OE *tūn*. Sometimes a Scandinavian termination replaced an original OE ending, as in **Holbeck** (Nt), 'hollow brook', the earliest form of which has OE *brōc*, instead of ON *bekkr*. In the frequent **Ashby** names, the opposite process has taken place; here ON *askr* (surviving in **Asby**, Cu, We) has been replaced by OE *æsc*. Other hybrids include **Cumberland** (British/OE) and **Haltwhistle**, Nb, 'high river-fork' (OF/OE *haut twisla*).

INVERSION COMPOUND

A name of Scandinavian origin, but Celtic in arrangement, placing the defining element (a personal name) last, e.g. **Brigsteer** (We), 'Styr's bridge'.

MANORIAL AFFIX

An addition to a place-name, indicating a former feudal tenant or lord of manor. The affix is often a surname, as in **Weston Beggard** (He), **Wootton Fitzpaine** (Do), **Woodham Ferrers** (E), **Weston Favell** (Nth), or **Walton Cardiff** (Gl). Sometimes it is a title, as in **Monks Risborough** (Bk) or **Princes Risborough** (Bk), 'brushwood-covered hill', held formerly by the monks of Christchurch, Canterbury, and the Black Prince, respectively.

NATURE-NAME

A place-name referring to a geographical feature, e.g. **Liverpool**, 'pool with thick water', **Brewood** (St), 'wood on the hill', **Iver** (Bk), 'steep slope', **Clee** (L), 'clay', and **Tring** (Hrt), 'tree-covered slope'. None of these contains an element indicating that the name actually refers to a settlement at or near the natural objects concerned.

POPULAR ETYMOLOGY

The interpretation of a place-name by the 'common-sense' method of giving the meaning of the present form of the name, e.g. by relating **Barking** (GL) to the **Isle of Dogs,** not far away. Another aspect of the process is the replacement of an unfamiliar, unpronounceable, or unintelligible name by something with which the users are more at home, as the replacement of the Cornish names *Coit-bran* ('crow wood') and *Pen-lestyn* ('chief lodging'), by **Cutbrawn** and **Palestine.**

SIMPLEX

A place-name consisting of a single element, e.g. **Barnes** (Sr), 'barns', **Bootle** (La), 'dwelling', **Ford** (He), 'ford', and **Stone** (St), 'stone', containing respectively OE *bere-ærn, bothl, ford,* and *stān.*

THEME

An ultimate significant component of personal names, place-name elements, etc. See COMPOUND.

TOPONYMY

The study of place-names. *Onomastics* is the term applied to the study of names in general.

TRANSFERRED NAME

A place-name already used of one locality deliberately transplanted elsewhere, e.g. **Richmond** (Sr), named after **Richmond** (NRY). The most spectacular example in England is **Baldock** (Hrt), which was named (by returning Crusaders) after **Baghdad.** There are, of course, numerous transferred names in USA, Canada, Australia, and New Zealand.

12: BOOKS AND ORGANISATIONS

For further reading

The best general introduction to English place-names is **K. Cameron:** *English Place-Names.* Also general, but containing detailed discussion of a number of important names, is **P. H. Reaney:** *The Origin of English Place-Names.* Indispensable for constant reference are **E. Ekwall:** *The Concise Oxford Dictionary of English Place-Names* and a recent joint work by **W. Nicolaisen, M. Gelling,** and **M. Richards:** *The Names of Towns and Cities in Britain.* The latter book, also in dictionary form, supplements rather than replaces Ekwall's great work, and includes Scotland and Wales within its scope. For a thorough discussion of particular names, the reader should turn to the appropriate county volumes of the English Place-Name Society's survey. So far, 51 volumes have been published, covering 25 counties. For place-names outside England, see **W. J. Watson:** *The History of the Celtic Place-names of Scotland,* **P. W. Joyce:** *Irish Names of Places,* **B. G. Charles:** *Non-Celtic Place-names of Wales,* and **J. J. Kneen:** *Place-names of the Isle of Man.* **C. M. Matthews:** *Place-names of the English-speaking World* is wider in scope, but includes much relevant information. Matters touched on in chapter 10 are treated in greater detail in **E. Ekwall:** *Street-names of the City of London* and **J. Field:** *English Field Names.*

Organizations

Organizations whose work may be of interest to readers of this book include:

The Names Society. This relatively new organization seeks to draw together everyone with every kind of interest in names of all types, including surnames and place-names. An informal and informative news-letter, the price of which is included in the annual subscription of £1.00, is published every two months. Applications for membership should be addressed to A. W. Jones, 57 Chessington Way, West Wickham, Kent.

The English Place-Name Society. For over fifty years this society has been surveying the place-names of England, county by county. The annual volumes are now highly regarded as authoritative sources of information, and every place-name enthusiast is urged to study the volume relating to his own area. The society also publishes an annual *Journal.* For details of membership apply to the Hon. Secretary, English Place-Name Society, School of English Studies, The University, Nottingham NG7 2RD.

INDEX OF PLACE-NAMES

The Index lists every place-name explained or mentioned. English names are followed by the county abbreviation as given in the Table of Abbreviations. Welsh county-names are given in full or abbreviated conventionally. Scottish names have the name of the county less *-shire;* similarly Irish names are followed usually by the county name in full, but not including prefixed *Co.*, when this is usual. Names of towns and cities which give their name to their counties are not followed by a county name or abbreviation. River-names are followed by the word *river* in parentheses, to avoid confusion with county-names.

48

Greatham, Du 15
Greetham, L 15
Grimethorpe, WRY 18
Grimsby, L 18
Grimston, *freq* 19
Grosmont, NRY, Mon 22
Gunnersbury, Mx 4, 16
Gunnerthwaite, La 19
Gusborne (river) 38
Gutterby, Cu 18
Gwent 29
Gwynedd 29

Haddington 36
Haltemprice, ERY 22
Haltwhistle, Nb 22, 42
Hamble le Rice, Ha 22
Hamilton, Lanark 36
Hampshire 6
Hampstead, Mx, Brk 15
Hampsthwaite, WRY 19
Hamstead, St, Wt
Hamsworthy, D 14
Hanger Hill, Nt 20
Harlech, Merioneth 29
Harraby, Cu 18
Harrow, Mx 12
Hartley, *freq* 16
Hartley Mauditt, Ha 24
Hastings, Sx 11
Haverfordwest, Pem 26
Havering, E 11
Haverthwaite, La 19
Hawarden, Flint 28
Hawthornthwaite, La 19
Hazelwick, Sx 13
Helmsdale, Sutherland 33
Hemel Hempstead, Hrt 15, 41
Hempstead, E, Nf 15
Henley, O 15
Hereford 12
Herstmonceux, Sx 24
Hertford 12
Hertingfordbury, Hrt 16
Highworth, W 13
Highworthy, D 13
Hill Chorlton, St 26
Hillborough, K 16
Hinton Admiral, Ha 23, 24
Hinxworth, Hrt 13
Holbeck, Nt 42
Holderness, ERY 19

Holland, L 7
Holme Pierrepont, Nt 24
Holyhead, Ang 27
Honeywick, Sx 13
Honington, Wa 14
Honiton, D 14
Horseley, *freq* 16
Houghton Conquest, Bd 23
Huish Episcopi, So 25
Humber (river) 37
Huntingdon 7, 13
Hurstpierpoint, Sx 24
Hutton le Hole, NRY 22

Ingardine, Sa 14
Ingleby, *freq* 18
Inverness 34
Ireland 29
Isle of Dogs, GL 43
Isleworth, Mx 13
Itterby, L 16
Iver, Bk 43

Jenningsbury, Hrt 4
Jervaulx, NRY 22
Jurby, IOM 29

Keddleston, Db 19
Keith, Banff 34
Kells, Meath 32
Kent 5
Kerry 32
Kesteven, L 7
Keswick, Cu 13
Kettlethorpe, WRY 18
Kildare 32
Kilkenny 31
Killarney, Kerry 31
Kinder Scout, Db 39
King's Cliffe, Nth 37
King's Norton, Wo 14
Kingsbury Episcopi, So 25
Kinsale, Cork 32
Kirby, *freq* 17
Kirkandrews, Cu 20
Kirkbride, IOM 29
Kirkby, *freq* 17
Kirkoswald, Cu 20
Kirriemuir, Angus 34

Lackenby, NRY 18
Lairg, Sutherland 33

52

ABBREVIATIONS

Bd	Bedfordshire	Mx	Middlesex
Brk	Berkshire	Nb	Northumberland
Bk	Buckinghamshire	Nf	Norfolk
C	Cambridgeshire	NRY	North Riding, Yorks
Ch	Cheshire	Nt	Nottinghamshire
Co	Cornwall	Nth	Northamptonshire
Cu	Cumberland	O	Oxfordshire
D	Devon	OE	Old English
Db	Derbyshire	OF	Old French
Do	Dorset	OIr	Old Irish
Du	Durham	ON	Old Norse
E	Essex	R	Rutland
ERY	East Riding, Yorks	Sa	Shropshire
Gl	Gloucestershire	Sf	Suffolk
GL	Greater London	So	Somerset
Ha	Hampshire	Sr	Surrey
He	Herefordshire	St	Staffordshire
Hrt	Hertfordshire	Sx	Sussex
Hu	Huntingdonshire	W	Wiltshire
K	Kent	Wa	Warwickshire
L	Lincolnshire	We	Westmorland
La	Lancashire	Wo	Worcestershire
Lei	Leicestershire	WRY	West Riding, Yorks
Mon	Monmouthshire	Wt	Isle of Wight

Some titles available in the 'Discovering' series

Antique Maps
Archaeology in Denmark
Archaeology in England and Wales
Avon
Banknotes
Battlefields of Scotland
Beekeeping
Bells and Bellringing
Bird Song
Bird Watching
Brasses and Brassrubbing
British Cavalry Regiments
British Ponies
Burns Country
Cambridgeshire
Carts and Wagons
Castle Combe
Castles in England and Wales
Cathedrals
Chapels and Meeting Houses
Cheshire
Chess
Christmas Customs and Folklore
Churches
Corn Dollies
Country Crafts
Craft of the Inland Waterways
Derbyshire and the Peak District
Ecology
Edged Weapons
Embroidery of the Nineteenth Century
English Dialects
English Folk Dance
English Furniture
English Literary Associations
Essex
Famous Battles: Peninsular War
Farm Museums and Farm Parks
Folklore and Customs of Love and Marriage
Folklore of Plants
French and German Military Uniforms
Gardening for the Handicapped
Geology
Hallmarks on English Silver
Hampshire and the New Forest
Herbs
Hill Figures
Horse Brasses
Horse-drawn Carriages
Horse-drawn Commercial Vehicles
Horse-drawn Transport of the British Army
Industrial Archaeology and History
Kent
Kings and Queens
Lakeland
Lancashire

Leicestershire and Rutland
Lincolnshire
Local History
London's Canals
London for Children
London Street Names
London Villages
Lost Canals
Lost Railways
Mah-jong
Mechanical Music
Military Traditions
Model Soldiers
Mottoes
Norfolk
Northamptonshire
Northumbria
Off-beat Walks in London
Old Aeroplanes
Old Bicycles
Old Motor Cycles
Pantomime
Picture Postcards
Place Names
Quantocks
Regional Archaeology series:
  North-Eastern England
  North-Western England
  South-Eastern England
  South-Western England
Rules for Wargaming
Salop
South Yorkshire
Space and Astronomy
Staffordshire
Stately Homes
Statues in Cent. & N. England
Statues in S. England
Suffolk
Surnames
Sussex
Thames and Chilterns
Theatre Ephemera
Topiary
Towns
Toys and Toy Museums
Trams and Tramways
Walks in Buckinghamshire
Walks in the Cotswolds
Walks in the New Forest
Walks in Wessex Towns
Walks in West Sussex
Watermills
Westward Stage
Windmills
Your Family Tree
Your Old House

From your bookseller or from Shire Publications Ltd, Cromwell House, Church Street, Princes Risborough, Aylesbury, Bucks, HP17 9AJ, U.K.